American Authors

Kai-yu Hsu

Helen Palubinskas

This book is for Roland.

"'Auntie Tsia Lays Dying,'" copyright © 1972 by Jeffery Chan.

"A Funeral," copyright © 1972 by Samuel Tagatac.

"It Was a Warm Summer Day," copyright © 1972 by Alfred Robles.

"Letter to Kay Boyle," copyright © 1972 by Shawn H. Wong.

"A Letter to Nancy" and "What We Know," copyright © 1972 by Bayani L. Mariano

"The Price," copyright © 1972 by Oscar F. Peñaranda.

"Query" and "Sphinx," copyright © 1972 by Joaquin Legaspi.

"The Room" and "San Bruno," copyright © 1972 by Iwao Kawakami.

"Threads," copyright © 1972 by Russell C. Leong.

Printed in the United States of America.

Library of Congress Catalog Card Number: 71–160037

ISBN: 0–395–12701–7

ACKNOWLEDGMENTS

The authors extend a special note of thanks to Elgin Heinz, Jeanne Horbach, Jean-Pierre Hsu, Po-tsou Hsu, Harry Honda, Nathan Lee, and Paula Norton for their help in the preparation of this text. The interviews referred to in the general introduction were secured by the Chinese-American Resources Project based in the San Francisco Bay area. For permission to use them, the authors are most grateful. Grateful acknowledgment is also made to authors, publishers, and agents for their permission to reprint the following selections.

"The Brown House," by Hisaye Yamamoto. Copyright 1951 by Hearst Magazines, Inc. First appeared in *Harper's Bazaar* in the October, 1951 issue. Reprinted by permission of the author.

"The Eggs of the World," from *Yokohama, California,* by Toshio Mori. Copyright 1949 by The Caxton Printers, Ltd., Caldwell, Idaho.

"Food for All His Dead," by Frank Chin. Copyright © 1962, 1967, 1971 by Frank Chin. Reprinted by permission of the author.

From *Father and Glorious Descendant,* by Pardee Lowe. Published by Little, Brown and Co. Copyright 1943, copyright © renewed 1971 by Pardee Lowe.

From *The Frontiers of Love.* Condensed from the book by Diana Chang. Copyright © 1956 by Diana Chang. Reprinted by permission of Random House, Inc.

From *The House that Tai Ming Built,* by Virginia Lee. Copyright © 1963 by Virginia Lee. Reprinted by permission of The Macmillan Company.

"A Measure of Freedom," from pages 121–133 in *Fifth Chinese Daughter,* by Jade Snow Wong. Copyright 1945, 1948, 1950 by Jade Snow Wong. Reprinted by permission of Harper & Row, Publishers, Inc.

"The Morning Star," from *Selected Stories,* by N. V. M. Gonzalez. Copyright © 1964 by N. V. M. Gonzalez. Reprinted by permission of The Swallow Press, Chicago.

"One Sunday in December," from the book *Journey to Washington,* by Daniel K. Inouye with Lawrence Elliott. Copyright © 1967 by Prentice-Hall, Inc.

"Poems 57 and 60," from *Have Come, Am Here,* Poems by José García Villa. Copyright 1941, 1942, copyright © renewed 1969, 1970 by José García Villa. Reprinted by permission of The Viking Press, Inc.

"Scent of Apples," reprinted from *You Lovely People,* by Bienvenido N. Santos, by permission of the author.

"A Summer in an Alaskan Salmon Cannery," by J. C. Dionisio. First appeared in *Philippine Magazine.* Reprinted by permission of the author.

"West Side Songs," by Lawson Fusao Inada, reprinted from *Down at the Santa Fe Depot: 20 Fresno Poets,* edited by David Kherdian and James Baloian, by permission of the publishers, The Giligia Press, Fresno, California.

PHOTO CREDITS

Page viii (Kai-yu Hsu), Jean-Pierre Hsu; p. 24, courtesy of Harper & Row, Inc.; p. 47, Frank B. Denman; p. 62, courtesy of Random House, Inc., photo by George Cserna; p. 88, Eric L. Leong; p. 94, Stephen Y. Mori; p. 108, David Powell; p. 142, California State *Daily Pioneer.*

Contents

About the Authors

KAI-YU HSU

Kai-yu Hsu is a professor of humanities, foreign languages, and world literature at San Francisco State College, where he directs the Carnegie Chinese Project and the Chinese Culture Text Project. He was graduated from the National Tsing Hua University of China and received his M.A. degree in journalism from the University of Oregon and his Ph.D. in modern Chinese literature and thought from Stanford University. Dr. Hsu has written for *The New York Times,* for the *Chinese World Daily,* and for the *Democratic Review* in Hong Kong and is the author of books on Chinese language, literature, and history, including *Chou En-lai: China's Gray Eminence.*

HELEN PALUBINSKAS

Since 1962 Helen Palubinskas has been working with young Asian-American students in San Francisco, using creative writing as a means of teaching English and self-expression. She has studied Chinese language and culture at National Cheng-chi University, Taipei, and at the University of Hawaii and the University of California at Berkeley. Mrs. Palubinskas attended Oberlin College and Western Reserve University and received a bachelor's degree from Boston University and a master's degree in English from San Francisco State College.

Authors may define the term Asian-American *in different ways. In this anthology every effort was made to represent the works of writers of Asian origin who have had extensive living experience in America. Those born and reared in America were considered first; then those who came to this country when very young and remained here. Although some of the Filipino writers presented here started their careers in the islands, they have been included because they established their reputations by writing and publishing in English, which was introduced to the Philippines by the Americans. Space limitations and other considerations have prevented the inclusion of Asian-American authors whose ethnic heritages lie beyond the shores of China, Japan, and the Philippines.*

Introduction

An Asian-American is first of all a man, just as a poet has to be human before being poetic. Yes? But no! says Frank Chin, author of "Food for All His Dead," when he disagrees with Virginia Lee, author of *The House that Tai Ming Built*, in an interview on August 2, 1970. Virginia Lee says that she is not so much concerned about being either Chinese or American or Chinese-American or American-Chinese as she is about being human. That's like saying you are a bean, says Frank Chin, one of the millions and billions of beans in the world, and not even a black or yellow bean at that. Where's your identity, then? snaps Frank in his radio-TV trained voice, clear, sure of his diction, eloquent in his delivery, and very much up-to-date with the slang of the young American—a bit hip, perhaps, but his whole manner communicating self-confidence and freedom from inhibition.

1

And Virginia cuts a figure in many ways just the opposite, and the contrast goes beyond the difference in sex. She is demure, pretty, feminine, her voice seductively soft with an all-American girl's accent which, if you put her behind a curtain, would suggest a willowy blonde whose every gesture and facial expression is cultivated and well calculated to appeal. I have no identity hang-ups, she declares, after first conceding that she has given some thought to the identity problem at one time or another in her life, but that it no longer bothers her.

But there *is* a problem, and it does bother, in different ways, all Asian-American writers. For that matter, the same problem disturbs all sensitive persons, regardless of their ethnic backgrounds. As Buddha so well recognized some twenty-five hundred years ago, before he reaches wisdom, man is never free from anxiety. He is always anxious to get something, or having gotten it, is worried about losing it. All his anxieties and worries result from his desiring something; he suffers because he has desires. And he has desires because he believes he can get something or hold on to something for *himself*. Buddha's formula for ending man's suffering is clear-cut and simple. The idea about one's self is an illusion, Buddha says, and the moment you can forget about yourself, you are already free. But we, being somewhat less than Buddha, cannot forget our "self"; hence the search—the perpetual search.

In the quiet and contented home of a one-culture family —such as surrounded the young Buddha in Nepal—the search is for an answer to who am I and what am I supposed to do and what does it mean to do and be such-and-such. The bicultural or cross-cultural person's problem is not any more profound, perhaps, but is that much more accentuated and brought to the fore by the dramatic forces, both surface and hidden, that operate on his experience.

To begin with the more obvious, there is the cultural, ethnic, social, and even political confrontation which often painfully victimizes and scars a bicultural person. In his autobiography, *Journey to Washington*, Daniel Inouye witnesses the rape of Pearl Harbor, and it drives him to become fiercely loyal to America, to throw himself repeatedly at the U.S. Army until he is accepted. He leaves an arm behind in the European theater. But he does so with the memory of how the haole (white) American boys at his Hawaiian high school have humiliated him as a "Jap." Toshio Mori romanticizes the relocation-center experience in his short stories and lives through World War II retaining his faith in this land of opportunity, but a tinge of sentimental nostalgia about his old Japanese village keeps him superimposing the image of Yokohama on his identification with San Leandro, California, where his parents had settled. And there are other vividly told stories about many Japanese-Americans torn between two ethnic, cultural, and political loyalties—so violently torn that it will be a long time before the survivors can feel whether they are alive or dead. For much of them is dead and perhaps can never be revived.

The World War II relocation-camp experience was painful. The U. S. Government ordered thousands of first-, second-, and even third-generation Japanese-Americans to leave their homes, abandon their businesses, and crowd into temporary quarters set up in places like the Tanforan racetrack near San Francisco and at Topaz, Utah, with very little advance warning. No less painful, however, was the earlier immigrants' suffering from racial discrimination at the hands of white Americans—the Bret Hartes,[1] and the Kearneys,[2] and the nondescript and unnamed neighborhood white boys who chanted "Ching Chong Chinaman" and "Fat Jap." Time and gradual socio-cultural enlightenment have modified much of the bitter hatred, but the scars are there to remind many Asian-Americans of an identity somehow separate from the mainstream of the white Americans.

In a less damaging but equally provocative way ethnic consciousness continues to be driven home to an Asian-

[1] BRET HARTES: Harte was a poet-journalist who referred to Chinese immigrants of the California gold-rush days as "the yellow heathens."
[2] KEARNEYS: Denis Kearney led a workingmen's protest movement, in the late nineteenth century, which opposed Chinese labor.

American. When Lawson Inada, a third-generation Japanese-American poet from Fresno, California, courts his brunette wife in Iowa, he is eyed by the ogling townspeople and country people and is frequently gnawed, or perhaps just nibbled, by his memory of the Massachusetts schoolchildren who whispered behind his back, "Look, a Jap teacher, a Jap teacher. . . ." Even a much sweeter sentiment can be provocative. When Jeff Chan, now teaching Asian-American literature at San Francisco State College, marries his white American girl, her folks go out of their way to be nice to him, taking him in as even more than a part of the family, and dote on his first child. But this serves to point up the ironic rejection demonstrated by his father, a totally Americanized and successful dentist who, without meaning to, reduces his communication with Jeff to zero.

On this level an Asian-American is reminded of his difference from a white American. Some Asian-Americans, including Virginia Lee, resent the difference, particularly in those moments when they embrace the American ideal of "regardless of race, religion, or national origin." Others, including Frank Chin, welcome it as something that sets them apart from the amorphous middle-class values of the "average American."

But the problem doesn't end there. Lawson Inada is, culturally, no more Japanese than the Black or Chicano living next door to his Fresno home. There is a beautiful culture over there, says Inada, but over there across the Pacific, and some day, not now, he may go to Japan and find out about it (just for a year, perhaps, says his wife Janet). Inada agrees with Frank Chin that the Asian cultures exhibited in Virginia Lee's or Toshio Mori's works are at best Asia's past seen through "white" eyes. They are the Asian images constructed and perpetuated by whites through outdated school textbooks; Chin and Inada have very little to do with them. They are the images of the soft exquisiteness of Chinese jade and the tranquil serenity of a Japanese miniature garden, of the meek, the harmonious, the family-bound and earth-bound, the wise, the introverted, the withdrawn.... Virginia Lee says, But aren't these still the majority of the Chinatown inhabitants? The rebellious and discontented, the Chinese hippies, she says, aren't they a very small minority in the minority community? But you are perpetuating the stereotype again, protests Frank Chin, and I want to do just the opposite; I want to torpedo the stereotype.

The rebellion against the stereotype is a real and serious undertaking of these Asian-American writers. They admit that they have responded to the impetus of the Black movement, but they recognize that their battle is their own, long overdue. They want Asian-Americans to be liked as they are: human beings with qualities of dignity and beauty, who happen to have skin of different hue, hair darker and straighter, speech accents uniquely their own. They want white Americans to accord respect to these traits without distorting them, coloring them, or romanticizing them. They want white Americans to see beauty in the brown and yellow, and respond to their language, Asian-American language, to its metaphors that may seem quaint or ungrammatical by a white American standard but that sensitively reflect their unique experience and mirror their world.

Above all, they want no more Oriental-houseboy image, no more quaint and exotic curio image, no more conversation-piece image, to be superimposed on them. Asian-American men want their masculinity recognized and responded to, fully and equally, by the white American female, and even more important, recognized and *respected* by the white American male. That's why you see the kind of symbolism developed in my new verses and stories, says Samuel Tagatac, a thirty-year-old Filipino poet brought up in southern California. He wants to reinstate the full-blooded human voice in his writing, the writing of a Filipino-American who has been culturally emasculated along with the Chinese- and Japanese-American for over one hundred years.

Of course, if Frank Chin and Virginia Lee represent two drastically different Asian-American world views, there are also other Asian-Americans whose search for identity has taken varied turns. The refreshing sensitivity in Shawn Wong's poems that speak in quite universal terms of man's joy and sorrow really reveals very little that is Asian-American; but he is writing to isolate blocks of his complex experiences and feelings, hoping to intensify and clarify them through the act of isolating them on paper, and ultimately to see more and know more of himself, an Asian-American. These verses must be me, Shawn Wong says, and if I have not ceased writing them, it means there is still more of me that cries to be written down and perceived, and I sense that there will be more and more of the Asian-American (that's me) emerging from my lines as time goes by.

And Oscar Peñaranda of the Filipino-American literature program at San Francisco State College, having spent half of the twenty-six years of his life here and half in the Philippines, expresses yet another common concern of a bicultural writer. Peñaranda has been trying to write about his Filipino experience in a language acquired in America, but he refuses to be categorized as an "Asian-American." His struggle is not so much one of identity as one of integrating the content with the form; he knows that any form he can give to his writing is also its content. Like C. Y. Lee (author of *Flower Drum Song*), Peñaranda feels no identity crisis, although Lee sees the problem in reverse. You people born in this country, says C. Y. Lee, ought to have no problem being assimilated into the American culture. Lee seems to feel that it is people like him who should be living through a perpetual identity crisis because they are Asian, typically and totally Asian, and yet are totally uprooted now in an *alien* country.

But the identity crisis is upon writers like Frank Chin and Lawson Inada, who hate the word *assimilation*. As Frank Chin sees it, C. Y. Lee can write without inhibition because he has adopted the white American medium and he knows he is Chinese, period. While Chin, speaking of himself, declares, "I am neither Chinese nor American; I'm a Chinaman."

CHINESE-AMERICAN LITERATURE

"Which I wish to remark,
  And my language is plain,
That for ways that are dark
  And for tricks that are vain,
The heathen Chinee is peculiar,
  Which the same I would rise to explain."

From "Plain Language from Truthful James"
by Bret Harte

"'Are we men?' says Joe Johnson, 'and list to this jaw,
Without process of warrant or color of law?
. . . .
'Shall we stand here as idle, and let Asia pour
Her barbaric hordes on this civilized shore?
Has the White Man no country? Are we left in the lurch?
And likewise what's gone of the Established Church?'"

From "The Latest Chinese Outrage"
by Bret Harte

It would be unfair to assume that Bret Harte described the early Chinese immigrants as yellow heathens who came to California in lust for gold just to set off the waves of anti-Chinese persecution that followed. But bloody persecutions did occur, whether because the Chinese were willing to work for longer hours at lower pay, thus constituting a job threat to the whites, or because the whites regarded the Chinese as dirty, base, and soulless, or for both reasons. Mistreatment of the Chinese spread like wildfire in the spring of 1876 when many of them were driven from small Western towns and mining camps by white mobs. In California, June of that year witnessed violence against the

Chinese in Truckee. The following March, rioters butchered five Chinese farmers in Chico, California. Four months later twenty-five Chinese laundry shops were burned in the Truckee area; the fleeing survivors met with bullets. Twenty-eight Chinese died in a massacre in 1885 in Rock Springs, Wyoming, where hundreds more had to abandon their homes, running for their lives. A similar wave of mass murders occurred in 1886 in Log Cabin, Oregon. . . .

An ominous beginning indeed for the Chinese-American experience of the last hundred years, and the bitter memory of it, amply stained in blood and tears, was repeatedly reinforced by the many immigration laws which singled out the Chinese for limitation and exclusion. These laws painfully affected the daily life of the Chinese in this country by reducing them to the status of second- or third-class citizens and tended to obscure the few generous American acts toward China. When a Chinese laundryman could not bring his family over from China, and hesitated to return to China himself for fear of being barred from re-entry, he had no interest in the news that American dollars went to relieve flood victims in eastern China.

Through the years most Chinese immigrants played the parts of silent sufferers, meek, uncomplaining, always hiding, always running away from trouble. The rare exceptions of rebellious individuals found themselves brought back into line, often not by the white government, but by their own elders in their tongs, family associations organized to help, protect, and police themselves. It was all a part of the old Chinese social tradition—the clan, through a single grand patriarch or a cluster of venerable elders, takes care of and keeps control over its members.

In San Francisco's Chinatown the major tongs banded together to create a super-authority known as the Six Companies. For years there has been an unofficial mayor ruling over the Big Port, as the Chinese in America call their adopted homeland in the Bay area. If a politician wanted to keep things quiet in Chinatown, he turned to this unofficial mayor whose orders went down the chain of command in the Six Companies. If the politician wanted to conduct a campaign for contributions, he again went through the

Six Companies. Later some Chinese learned to vote, and the politician sought support from them, again through the Six Companies.

The Six Companies thus became the machinery of social control among the Chinese-Americans and a symbol of the Chinese establishment, representing business interests whose chances lay in their cooperation with the larger establishment of the whites beyond Chinatown. Even long after the Six Companies had lost much of its formidable stature, because many American-born Chinese developed their careers away from Chinatown, those dissatisfied with the ghetto aspects of Chinatown continued to blame the Six Companies. The Six Companies butters up the white establishment and whitewashes the ghetto conditions here, declare the Wah Ching, a vociferous group of young Chinese who, like young Blacks, feel that they are the victims of racism in America. The Six Companies wants to go on with business-as-usual, sponsoring the Chinatown beauty contests and New Year dragon dances; the Wah Chings see these as acts of prostituting Chinatown to curry favor from white tourists. The confrontation exploded when some Wah Chings tried to burn the prancing colorful dragon in the 1969 New Year celebration.

From Bret Harte's yellow heathens to the angry young Wah Chings, the Chinese-American experience has been well chronicled by journalists and participants in such experiences, some of whom, though few, are Chinese born in America. But when Betty Lee Sung did research for her book *Mountain of Gold,* her arduous quest for shining examples of Chinese-Americans who made good netted only one man of letters, Lin Yutang, who is Chinese and has studied and lived in America but is not Chinese-American.

Why haven't more Chinese-Americans described their experience in fiction, sung it in poetry, and dramatized it in the theater? The first-generation immigrants understandably had their language difficulty, even in their mother tongue, since most of them had no chance for literary cultivation before their arrival in the Old Gold Mountain, another name given to San Francisco by those of them who came to California during the gold-rush days. After their arrival they were kept busy laboring eighteen to twenty hours a day to earn their livelihood and worrying about and fleeing from their white tormentors and immigration officials, not to speak of unscrupulous fellow-Chinese exploiters, during what was left of the night. Breaking away from the Chinatowns has consumed much of the second generation's creative energy, and the rest of it has been devoted to pursuits of middle-class American values: a surer way to make money and, through financial security, gain social status equal to that of the middle-class white American. Hence there is no lack of Chinese-American doctors and lawyers and engineers, but there are few writers.

The few Chinese-Americans who started writing imaginatively about their experiences followed the path of development of many writers—autobiographical at the beginning. In *Father and Glorious Descendant* and *Fifth Chinese Daughter*, Pardee Lowe and Jade Snow Wong did just that in 1943 and 1945 and, unfortunately, no more. Twenty years elapsed, twenty years of vacuum, until Virginia Lee's *The House that Tai Ming Built*, which is still semi-autobiographical. There is nothing wrong with autobiography—except when one realizes that the perceptions of reality revealed through these works seem to confirm rather than modify a stereotyped image of the Chinese and their culture. These largely autobiographical works tend to suggest the Chinese culture described in the connoisseurs' manuals of Chinese jade or oolong tea, and the stereotype of the Chinese immigrant, either withdrawn and totally Chinese, or quietly assimilated and unobtrusively American, a model of the results of the melting-pot process. Yet all these three books have a rightful claim to be landmarks in Chinese-American literature because, as Virginia Lee said in 1970, the authors wrote about the Chinese in America as they saw and understood them. Other Chinese-American writers, if they have different perceptions, should come forth with their stories.

There *are* different perceptions, and different Chinese-American stories are appearing. Between the extremes of the Chinese who have remained totally Chinese and the Chinese who have gone totally American, there is a wide spectrum of Americans of Chinese ancestry whose sensitivity is sharpened by their awareness of a "Chinatown culture" in their background which is neither Chinese nor American. When Frank Chin declares, "I'm just a China-man," it is not merely an expression of defiance. When Shawn Wong finally hears a Chinese-American voice in his own verse, it is not just because of the fad of the time. These younger authors and their contemporaries are struggling with considerable success to record what they see and feel—the tears and laughter and subtler moods in between of the real Chinaman of the 1970s. The events they describe reveal a deeper layer of human drama than a Chinatown police blotter shows. The characters they portray come closer to reality than Fu Manchu or the Number Two Son in *Flower Drum Song*. Theirs is what they choose to call, for lack of a more convenient term, a unique Chinese-American literary sensibility.

One way to understand this literary sensibility is to recognize the psychological and linguistic block that has hampered a number of Chinese-American writers. Without knowing it, many of them are accepting the image which the white Americans have assigned to the Chinese, thus perpetuating the mythical Chinese character of "keeping to themselves and keeping their place" as a virtue. Subconsciously they are living this virtue, thus expecting little of themselves or their fellow Chinese-Americans. For a Chinese to try to become an established creative writer in English is almost impossible, so states the myth, which is reinforced to some extent by the white-dominated writers' world in America. When C. Y. Lee, himself not exactly a Chinese-American, was struggling to break into the creative-writing market in the early 1950s before he hit it right with his *Flower Drum Song*, he was advised more than once to use a pen name to hide his Chinese identity!

With so much against them, it is small wonder that there have been and are any Chinese-Americans who have tried creative writing at all.

There is a still subtler psychological and linguistic handicap confronting the Chinese-American writer who wants to find himself and tell truthfully about himself. Language is inseparable from culture and inevitably reflects the norms of cultural values. When a Chinese-American tries to write in the white American language, he cannot easily escape from its stubborn, built-in tendency to mirror white American norms which drown out anything non-American. Pardee Lowe, Jade Snow Wong, and Virginia Lee are not conscious of this problem, but Frank Chin and his contemporaries are. The solution is not simple. Unlike the American Blacks who have more or less demonstrated that their speech can be effective in literature, Frank Chin and his writer friends are still sweating with the Chinatown speech to make it do serious work, sounding not like a comic caricature of the Ching Chong Chinaman, but like the real Chinaman, in flesh and blood, sharing the tragicomic fate of mankind with as much wisdom and depth of feeling as the greatest of men anytime, anywhere.

A Brief Chronology of the Chinese in America

1785　First record of Chinese in the eastern United States. Three Chinese and 32 East Indian seamen were abandoned in Baltimore by an American ship's captain. Later, in 1796, five Chinese servants were brought to Philadelphia by a retired Dutch merchant.

1790　Naturalization Act passed, limiting the right of citizenship to "free whites."

1820　First official record of Chinese immigration. Forty-three immigrants were recorded before 1849.

1849　In this year the Chinese population of San Francisco rose sharply, from 54 to 787 men and two women and increased to 4,018 in 1850. On December 10, 1849, about 300 Chinese met to ask Selim Woodworth to be their liaison person with the white community. Most of the Chinese were merchants with enterprises scattered throughout the city; a segregated Chinatown had not yet been established.

1852   San Francisco's first Chinese theater established. The building was brought from China.

1854   San Francisco's first Chinese newspaper published.

1858–1862   Chinese Six Companies formed (exact date uncertain). Associations of men who had come from various districts near Canton in China joined to form the organization. The Six Companies was their agency for arbitration, social welfare, and community interests. It was incorporated in 1901 as the Chinese Consolidated Benevolent Association, but the old popular name remained in circulation.

1868   Official Chinese restriction on persons wanting to to go to the United States removed.

1869   Completion of the transcontinental railroad. The western part was built largely with Chinese labor.

1870   Peak of Chinese mining activity.

1860s–1880s   Movement of Chinese laborers into agriculture, land reclamation, fishing, manufacturing, and service industries. Success in each of these fields was followed by anti-Chinese violence and restrictive legislation.

1878   Ch'en Lan-pin appointed Minister to the United States to protect Chinese laborers and students.

1882   Chinese Exclusion Act passed. This act was the culmination of a series of local anti-Chinese laws, most of which had been declared unconstitutional in test cases brought to court by individuals willing to fight for their civil rights.

1885   Yick Wo, convicted of operating a laundry without a license, took his case to the Supreme Court, which found, according to the wording of the decision, that "the law was administered with an evil eye" to drive Chinese out of business; the law was struck down as discriminatory. This was a key case in defining the 14th Amendment.

1902 Chinese Exclusion Act extended indefinitely.

1906 San Francisco Oriental School Segregation ruling. Pupils of oriental origin were barred from attending San Francisco schools, but this ruling was rescinded after five months.

1915 Chinese-American Citizens Alliance founded. An attempt at protecting the civil rights of Chinese-Americans, the alliance was developed from the Native Sons of the Golden State, a fraternal order founded by Chun Dick in 1895. It was psychologically significant in indicating the shift of commitment from *Chinese*-American to Chinese-*American*.

1920 Chinese-American population had declined from 132,000 to 61,639.

1935 *The Chinese Digest* founded. This was the first periodical published by a staff composed entirely of American-born Chinese.

1943 Repeal of the Chinese Exclusion Act.

1957 Nobel Prize in physics awarded to Tsung-dao Lee and Chen-nin Yang for "breaking" the conservation-of-parity law.

1965 National-origins quota system for immigration repealed, to take effect July 1, 1968.

Pardee Lowe

b. 1905

Pardee Lowe's father came to America at the age of twelve but later returned to his home town in South China to take a bride. He was never impressed by Christianity but caught early an intense fever of republicanism, American style. Thus his son was named after the then governor of California (George C. Pardee) to affirm his propitious birth, which fell on the anniversary of the state's Admission Day. Like many other successful Chinese immigrants in this country, the senior Lowe became a prosperous merchant through hard work plus an ample measure of stubborn will to succeed and a better-than-average aptitude for English. Also, like many other first-generation immigrants, he wanted his firstborn son to inherit his business.

Pardee Lowe was graduated from a high school in East Belleville, across the bay from San Francisco, where the family had moved after the 1906 earthquake made Chinatown unfit to live in. A no-interest student loan, much encouragement from his teachers, and Pardee Lowe's own argument persuaded his father to let him go to Stanford University, and later the Harvard Graduate School of Business Administration.

No amount of Pardee Lowe's academic advancement was enough to prepare his father for the shock of his son's return to California in 1932 with an American wife whom he had married the year before in Germany without notifying his parents. The senior Lowe never quite forgave him for that until the young man had the distinction of being invited, in 1935, to join the International Secretariat of the Institute of Pacific Relations—where he associated with many intellectual and political leaders of the world—

15

and three years later was placed in a leadership position in the China War Relief organizations throughout the country.

Parts of Father and Glorious Descendant *began to appear in the* Yale Review *and other leading journals around 1940, and together these chapters record Pardee Lowe's reminiscences of his father and the relationship between the patriarch and the rest of the family. The picture of the father may be somewhat overidealized, but the disillusionment described in the following pages certainly has been taken seriously by, and continues to cause great concern among, Asian-Americans.*

FROM
Father and Glorious Descendant

A few days after our return from the Sierra Nevada, father said gently, "Glorious Descendant, how would you like to go to a private boarding school in China?"

I shuddered at the full significance of his suggestion. To be separated from America and from my family? And never to see them again for years and years? "No! no!" I wailed. "I don't want to go!" Rejecting the idea with all the vehemence at my command, I added, "I want to stay in America!"

Father dwelt patiently on all the advantages of such a schooling, but to no avail. Nothing he said moved me. What about my future, inquired father; didn't I care? Of course, I replied, but I didn't want to be a mandarin[1] or a Chinese merchant prince at such a terrific sacrifice. Father's questions became more penetrating; they stripped the future of everything but realities. Could I, as a Chinese, ever hope to find a good job in American society? At this, I

[1] MANDARIN (măn′də·rĭn): high-ranking civil servant.

laughed. Miss McIntyre,[2] I told him, had plainly said that I could even be President.

In these sessions, I revealed to father the seriousness of my infection. I opened the gates to that part of my youthful life he had never known. I told him in no uncertain terms that I loved America, particularly East Belleville, which I considered to be the grandest place in all the world. Besides, I continued, why would I wish to go to China? All the things I had heard from our kinsfolk about the old country were bad, with no redeeming features. After all, I added as my clinching argument, if this were not so, why should our kinsmen wish to come to the United States?

Our cousins and uncles, father tried desperately to explain, really wanted to stay at home with their wives and children, but because times seemed so difficult in China, they were compelled, by economic necessity, to come and work in the Golden Mountains. "Don't think you're the only one who loves his family and hates to leave it," concluded father somewhat angrily.

The argument became endless. The more father pleaded, the more determined I became. America, I swore, was God's own country. It abounded in free public schools, libraries, newspapers, bathtubs, toilets, vaudeville theaters, and railroad trains. On the other hand, I reminded him, China was a place where anything might happen: one might be kidnaped, caught in a revolution, die from the heat, perish from the cold, or even pick up ringworm diseases which left huge bald patches on one's scalp.

Finally father was convinced. Since I did not personally regard his idea with favor, trying to send me to China was hopeless. This by no means exhausted father's remedial efforts on my behalf. Plan number one having failed, father put number two into operation. He decided that if I wouldn't go to China, I was to spend an extra hour each day on my Chinese studies for Tutor Chun.

Now I knew leisure no longer. My American playmates, and endless trips to the settlement library, were given up—but not forgotten. And I discovered to my painful sorrow that I had only substituted one necessary evil

[2] MISS McINTYRE: one of the young Pardee's public-school teachers.

for another. Every evening from five to eight I despon-
dently memorized, recited, and copied endless columns
of queer-shaped characters which bore not the slightest
resemblance to English. As I went to this school on Saturday mornings and studied my lessons on Sunday, I envied
Penelope, Heinz, and Francisco, my poorest foreign playmates, their luxurious freedom. They did not have to learn
Chinese.

Unlike my American education, my Chinese one was not
crowned with success. It was not that I was entirely unwilling to learn, but simply that my brain was not ambi-
dextrous. Whenever I stood with my back to the teacher,
my lips attempted to recite correctly in poetical prose
Chinese history, geography, or ethics, while my inner
spirit was wrestling victoriously with the details of the
Battle of Bunker Hill, Custer's Last Stand, or the tussle
between the *Monitor* and *Merrimac*.

When it became apparent to Tutor Chun that in spite of
my extra hour a day, I was unable to balance cultural
waters on both shoulders, he mercifully desisted flailing
me with the bamboo duster. No amount of chastising, he
informed me bitterly, would ever unravel the cultural chop
suey I was making of my studies. But in the long run, even
the gentle soul of the Chinese teacher could not tolerate
my muddleheadedness. One day, after a particularly heart-
rending recitation on my part, he telephoned mother in
despair. "Madame," he exclaimed in mortal anguish,
"never have I had a pupil the equal of your son. I strain
all my efforts, but alas, I profoundly regret that I am unable
to teach him anything!"

Father was appalled at this news, but since he was not
the kind of man who gave up easily, his determination
waxed all the stronger. Subtler methods, bribery, were
tried. Perhaps, he reasoned, I might develop a taste for
Chinese as well as English literature if it were only made
financially worth my while. Each Sunday a shining quarter
would be mine, he said, if I would present him with a daily
ten-minute verbal Chinese translation of the latest newspaper reports on European war developments.

Lured by this largess, I made my translations. They were,

to be sure, crude and swiftly drawn. But then, ten minutes was all too brief a period in which to circumnavigate the globe and report on its current events. I endowed the military movements of von Kluck's, Foch's, and Haig's armies with the élan[3] of Sheridan's sweep down the Shenandoah, unencumbered with the intricate mechanized paraphernalia of modern warfare. And long before Wilson, Clemenceau, and Lloyd George assembled at Versailles, I had made and remade the map of Europe a dozen times.

Father's clever scheme not only worked, but it proved mutually beneficial. During the four years of the war, we kept it up. Thanks to the revolutionary *Young China,* and the *Christian Chinese Western Daily,* he was never entirely in the dark as to which armies won which campaign and who finally won the war. Naturally, father learned a great deal about history that wasn't so, but he did not particularly mind. I was improving my Chinese.

During this period my youthful cup of patriotism was filled to overflowing. In the first place our Americanism had finally reached the ears of the White House. The christening of my twin brothers brought two important letters of congratulation from Washington, which father proudly framed and hung conspicuously in his private office. As might be imagined, they exerted a profound influence on all our lives.

When I felt particularly in need of encouragement, I would go to the back wall of father's office and read aloud Vice President Marshall's letter to father. It was a human one, glowing with warmth and inspiration. There was one sentence which stood out: "To be a good American citizen, in my judgment, is about the best thing on earth, and while I cannot endow your children with any worldly goods, I can bless them with the hope that they may grow up to be an honor to their parents and a credit to the commonwealth."

I recall this Vice-Presidential blessing so vividly because it was the crux of our family problem. It summed up our difficulties as well as our goal. For me, at least, it was difficult to be a filial Chinese son and a good American citizen at one and the same time. For many years I used to

[3] ÉLAN (ā·län'): enthusiasm; style.

wonder why this was so, but I appreciate now it was because I was the eldest son in what was essentially a pioneering family. Father was pioneering with Americanism—and so was I. And more often than not, we blazed entirely different trails.

When America finally entered the war, even father's sturdy common sense softened somewhat under the heat waves of patriotism that constantly beat down upon us. I was in paradise. My youthful fancies appreciated that only strife and turmoil made heroes. When I recalled that practically every great President—Washington, Jackson, Lincoln, Grant, and Roosevelt—had once been a soldier, I bitterly lamented the fact that I was not old enough. I'd show those "Huns" (by this time I had already imbibed freely at the fount of propaganda) a thing or two, I informed father. But father only snorted something about waiting until I could shoulder a gun, and studying Chinese.

The next summer, my thirteenth, I decided to go to work during vacation. I needed spending money badly for my first term in high school. Father applauded this show of independence until I informed him that I intended, if possible, to become an office boy in an American business firm. Then he was seized with profound misgivings. "Would they hire you?" father inquired.

Why shouldn't they, I replied, with overweening self-confidence. "See!" I pointed to the Sunday editions of the *San Francisco Chronicle*. "I can hold any of these jobs."

Father looked at the classified advertisements I had checked. Whether he knew what all the abbreviations meant, I wasn't certain. I didn't, but that was totally immaterial. The world was new, I was young, and for $40 a month I was willing to learn the ins. or exp. bus., work for good opps., be ready to asst. on files, and, for good measure, do gen. off. wk. for perm. adv.

Father remarked that he wasn't so certain that the millennium[4] had arrived, but he was open to conviction. He agreed to let me proceed on one condition: if I failed to find a job, I was to return to Tutor Chun and study my Chinese lessons faithfully.

[4] MILLENNIUM (mə·lĕn'ē·əm): time of perfection in human existence.

Blithely one sunny July morning I went forth job hunt-
ing, well-scrubbed, wearing my Sunday suit, and totally
unaware of the difficulties that confronted me. In my
pocket were ten clipped newspaper advertisements, each
one, I thought, with a job purposely made for me.

I took out the most promising one. It was for seven
enterp. boys, between the ages of 12 and 16; and they were
wanted at once for a bond house which offered good opps.
as well as $50 per month. The address was on California
Street.

Stopping in front of an imposing marble palace of San
Francisco finance, I compared the address with the clip-
ping. It checked. How simply grand it would be to work for
such a firm, I thought, as the elevator majestically pulled us
up to the ninth floor. I trembled with eager anticipation
as I pushed open the glass door of Richards and Mathison,
for it seemed as though a new world were swimming into
view.

"Wad-a-ya-wunt?" barked the sharp voice of a young
lady. I looked in her direction. There she sat behind a
shiny, thin brass cage, just like a bank teller—or a monkey,
for above her head hung a sign. It read INFORMATION.

"Please, ma'am," I asked, "can you tell me where I can
find Mr. Royal?"

"Humph!" she snorted, as she looked me up and down
as if to say I didn't have a chance. "He's busy; you'll have
to wait."

After what seemed hours, the girl threw open the office
gate and motioned me to enter. I followed her down a long
aisle of desks, every one as large as a kitchen table. At each
desk sat a man or a girl shuffling large cards or scribbling
on long sheets of paper. As we passed, they stopped their
work and looked at me queerly. I noticed several boys of
my own age putting their heads together. I knew they were
talking about me. And when they snickered, I wanted to
punch their noses.

Opening a door marked PRIVATE, the girl announced:
"Mr. Royal, here is another boy." He raised his head.

There it was. On Mr. Royal's lean, smooth-shaven face
was the same look of incredulity. . . . But only for a moment.

For he suddenly reached for a cigarette, lit it, and looked at me quizzically, while I hopped on one foot and then on the other.

"Young man," he said, "I understand you would like to work for us? Well then, you'd better tell us something of yourself."

"Why, of course," I said, "of course." And impulsively I told everything: all about my graduation from grammar school, my boy-scout training, and my desire to earn my own keep during the summer.

Mr. Royal seemed visibly impressed. When a faint smile replaced his frown, I stopped fidgeting. I fully expected him to ask me to come to work in the morning. Therefore, I was appalled when he told me that he was sorry, but all the jobs were taken. It never occurred to me that our interview would end like this.

My face fell. I hadn't expected such an answer. To soften the blow, Mr. Royal added that if I filled out an application, he would call me if there were any openings.

I filled out the application under the unsympathetic eyes of the information girl and stumbled miserably out of the office, vaguely sensible of the fact that there would never be any opening.

The feeling was intensified as I made the round of the other nine firms. Everywhere I was greeted with perturbation, amusement, pity, or irritation—and always with identically the same answer. "Sorry," they invariably said, "the position has just been filled." My jaunty self-confidence soon wilted. I sensed that something was radically, fundamentally wrong. It just didn't seem possible that overnight all of the positions could have been occupied, particularly not when everybody spoke of a labor shortage. Suspicion began to dawn. What had father said? "American firms do not customarily employ Chinese." To verify his statement, I looked again in the newspaper the next morning and for the week after, and sure enough, just as I expected, the same ten ads were still in the newspaper.

For another week, I tried my luck. By now I was thoroughly shellshocked. What had begun as a glorious adventure had turned into a hideous, long-drawn nightmare.

Father during this trying period wisely said nothing. Then, one morning, he dusted off my dog-eared paperbound Chinese textbooks. When I came to breakfast, I found them on my desk, mute but eloquent reminders of my promise. I looked at them disconsolately. A bargain was a bargain.

When our clock struck nine, I picked up my bundle of books. Fortunately for me, father had already commuted to work. Only mother saw me off. Patting me sympathetically on the shoulder, she regarded me reflectively. It was an invitation for me to unburden my heart. But not even for her would I confess my full recovery from a nearly fatal disease. That moment was reserved for my long walk to language school.

I marched out of the house insouciant.[5] When I wasn't whistling, I was muttering to myself a Jewish slang phrase I had just picked up. It was "Ishkabibble" and it meant that I didn't care. And I didn't until I reached the park where all my most vivid daydreaming periods were spent. There, I broke down and wept. For the first time I admitted to myself the cruel truth—I didn't have a "Chinaman's chance" of becoming President of the United States. In this crash of the lofty hopes which Miss McIntyre had raised, it did not occur to me to reflect that the chances of Francisco Trujillo, Yuri Matsuyama, or Penelope Lincoln were actually no better than mine. But after a good cry I felt better—anyway, I could go to an American school again in the fall.

[5] INSOUCIANT (ĭn·sōō′sē·ənt): in a lighthearted, unconcerned manner.

FOR DISCUSSION

1. Why was it difficult for Pardee Lowe "to be a filial Chinese son and a good American citizen at one and the same time"? Do any similar conflicts exist today?

2. The author relates an experience with job discrimination which occurred in 1918. Can you offer any evidence which supports or refutes claims that such job discrimination exists today?

Jade Snow Wong

b. 1922

Struggle against being considered just another obedient child among her brothers and sisters, against racial prejudice visited upon her since childhood, against sexual discrimination enforced by family tradition that preferred the male offspring, against parental authoritarianism, and finally against herself in an effort to find meaning for her own life—these are the tensions described in Jade Snow Wong's autobiographical novel Fifth Chinese Daughter.

If most of these problems were shared by the majority of Chinese-Americans of her generation, the last, the struggle to find oneself, reveals more of Jade Snow Wong the individual. At one point in her novel, she identifies with China and the Chinese people, convinced that she can find meaning for her life only if she renders services to China, a conviction reinforced later by her American professor of sociology at college. However, when she formulates a long-range plan for her adult life several years later, ethnic consideration becomes subordinate to her determination to give expression to her inner self, and form to her creative energy. Thus there is a note of irony when, toward the very end of the book, she acknowledges her success as a fulfillment of her father's traditional Chinese dream of seeing his daughter "make good" and "get ahead" in social and worldly terms.

A second-generation Chinese-American, Jade Snow Wong got her name because her birth coincided with the rare occurrence of snow in the San Francisco area, an event which impressed her mother deeply. She was graduated from Mills College in 1942, worked for the navy during the remainder of World War II, and soon after that started making and selling ceramics in San Francisco.

A Measure of Freedom

So, without much enthusiasm, Jade Snow decided upon junior college. Now it was necessary to inform mama and daddy. She chose an evening when the family was at dinner. All of them were in their customary places, and daddy, typically, was in conversation with Older Brother about the factory:

"Blessing, when do you think Lot Number fifty-one twenty-six will be finished? I want to ask for a check from our jobber so that I can have enough cash for next week's payroll."

To which Older Brother replied, "As soon as mama is through with the seams in Mrs. Lee's and Mrs. Choy's bundles, the women can finish the hems. Another day, probably."

Mama had not been consulted; therefore, she made no comment. Silence descended as the Wongs continued their meal, observing the well-learned precept that talk was not permissible while eating.

Jade Snow considered whether to break the silence. Three times she thought over what she had to say, and still found it worth saying. This also was according to family precept.

"Daddy," she said, "I have made up my mind to enter junior college here in San Francisco. I will find a steady job to pay my expenses, and by working in the summers I'll try to save enough money to take me through my last two years at the university."

Then she waited. Everyone went on eating. No one said a word. Apparently no one was interested enough to be curious. But at least no one objected. It was settled.

Junior college was at first disappointing in more ways than one. There was none of the glamor usually associated with college because the institution was so young that it had not yet acquired buildings of its own. Classes were held all over the city, wherever accommodations were available. The first days were very confusing to Jade Snow,

25

especially when she discovered that she must immediately decide upon a college major.

While waiting to register, she thumbed through the catalogue in search of a clue. English . . . mathematics . . . chemistry. . . . In the last semester of high school she had found chemistry particularly fascinating; so with a feeling of assurance she wrote that as her major on the necessary forms and went to a sign-up table.

"I wish to take the lecture and laboratory classes for Chemistry 1A," she informed the gray-haired man who presided there.

He looked at her, a trifle impatiently, she thought.

"Why?"

"Because I like it." To herself she sounded reasonable.

"But you are no longer in high school. Chemistry here is a difficult subject on a university level, planned for those who are majoring in medicine, engineering, or the serious sciences."

Jade Snow set her chin stubbornly. "I still want to take Chemistry 1A."

Sharply he questioned: "What courses in mathematics have you had? What were your grades?"

Finally Jade Snow's annoyance rose to the surface. "Straight A's. But why must you ask? Do you think I would want to take a course I couldn't pass? Why don't you sign me up and let the instructor be the judge of my ability?"

"Very well," he replied stiffly. "I'll accept you in the class. And for your information, young lady, I am the instructor!"

With this inauspicious start, Jade Snow began her college career.

To take care of finances, she now needed to look for work. Through a friend she learned that a Mrs. Simpson needed someone to help with household work. "Can you cook?" was Mrs. Simpson's first question.

Jade Snow considered a moment before answering. Certainly she could cook Chinese food, and she remembered a common Chinese saying, "A Chinese can cook foreign food as well as, if not better than, the foreigners, but a foreigner cannot cook Chinese food fit for the Chinese." On this reasoning it seemed safe to say "Yes."

After some further discussion Jade Snow was hired. Cooking, she discovered, included everything from pastries, puddings, meats, steaks, and vegetables, to sandwiches. In addition, she served the meals, washed dishes, kept the house clean, did the light laundry and ironing for Mr. and Mrs. Simpson and their career daughter—and always appeared in uniform, which she thoroughly disliked. In return she received twenty dollars a month. At night, she did her studying at home, and sometimes after a hard day she was so tired that the walk from the Simpson flat to the streetcar on Chestnut Street was a blessed respite, a time to relax and admire the moon if she could find it, and to gather fresh energy for whatever lay ahead.

Desserts, quite ignored in a Chinese household, were of first importance in the Simpson household. One particular Saturday, Jade Snow was told to bake a special meringue sponge cake with a fancy fruit filling of whipped cream and peeled and seeded grapes. Following a very special recipe of Mrs. Simpson's, she mixed it for the first time and preheated the oven. Mrs. Simpson came into the kitchen, checked and approved the prepared cake batter, and said that she would judge when it was done. Meantime she and her husband and their guests lounged happily in the garden.

Almost an hour passed. The meringue was baking in a slow oven. The recipe said not to open the door, as the cake might fall. An hour and a quarter passed, and the pastry smelled sweetly delicate. Yet Mrs. Simpson did not come. Jade Snow wondered whether or not to call her. But she remembered that her employer disliked being disturbed when entertaining officials of her husband's company.

After an hour and forty-five minutes the cake no longer smelled delicate. Jade Snow was worn out! What could she do? At last, there was a rush of high-heeled footsteps; swish went the kitchen door, and Mrs. Simpson burst in, flushed from the sun or excitement.

"I must look at that meringue cake," she burst out.

The oven door was pulled open, and Jade Snow peered in anxiously over her employer's shoulder. Too late! It had fallen and become a tough, brown mass. Jade Snow was dumb with a crushed heart, inspecting the flattened pancake, mentally reviewing all the processes of whipping, measuring, and sifting that she had gone through for hours to achieve this unpalatable result.

Mrs. Simpson crisply broke through to her anguish, "Well, there's nothing to be done but for you to make another."

That afternoon was a torturous nightmare and a fever of activity—to manage another meringue cake, to get rolls mixed, salad greens cleaned and crisped, vegetables cut, meat broiled, the table set, and all of the other details of a "company" dinner attended to. By the time she was at last washing the dishes and tidying the dining room, she felt strangely vague. She hadn't taken time to eat her dinner; she was too tired anyway. How she wished that she had been asked to cook a Chinese dinner instead of this interminable American meal, especially that cake!

Of her college courses, Latin was the easiest. This was a surprise, for everyone had told her of its horrors. It was much more logical than French, almost mathematical in its orderliness and precision, and actually a snap after nine years of Chinese.

Chemistry, true to the instructor's promise, was difficult, although the classes were anything but dull. It turned out that he was a very nice person with a keen sense of humor and a gift for enlivening his lectures with stories of his own college days. There were only two girls in a class of more than fifty men—a tense blonde girl from Germany, who always ranked first; and Jade Snow, who usually took second place.

But if Latin was the easiest course and chemistry the most difficult, sociology was the most stimulating. Jade Snow had chosen it without thought, simply to meet a requirement; but that casual decision completely revolutionized her thinking, shattering her Wong-constructed conception of the order of things. This was the way it happened:

After several uneventful weeks during which the class explored the historical origins of the family and examined such terms as *norms, mores, folkways,* there came a day when the instructor stood before them to discuss the relationship of parents and children. It was a day like many others, with the students listening in varying attitudes of interest or indifference. The instructor was speaking casually of ideas to be accepted as standard. Then suddenly upon Jade Snow's astounded ears there fell this statement:

"There was a period in our American history when parents had children for economic reasons, to put them to work as soon as possible, especially to have them help on the farm. But now we no longer regard children in this way. Today we recognize that children are individuals, and that parents can no longer demand their unquestioning obedience. Parents should do their best to understand their children, because young people also have their rights."

The instructor went on talking, but Jade Snow heard no more, for her mind was echoing and re-echoing this startling thought. "Parents can no longer demand unquestioning obedience from their children. They should do their best to understand. Children also have their rights." For the rest of the day, while she was doing her chores at the Simpsons', while she was standing in the streetcar going home, she was busy translating the idea into terms of her own experience.

"My parents demand unquestioning obedience. Older Brother demands unquestioning obedience. By what right? I am an individual besides being a Chinese daughter. I have rights too."

Could it be that daddy and mama, although they were living in San Francisco in the year 1938, actually had not left the Chinese world of thirty years ago? Could it be that they were forgetting that Jade Snow would soon become a woman in a new America, not a woman in old China? In short, was it possible that daddy and mama could be wrong?

For days Jade Snow gave thought to little but her devastating discovery that her parents might be subject to error. As it was her habit always to act after reaching a conclusion, she wondered what to do about it. Should she tell daddy and mama that they needed to change their ways? One moment she thought she should; the next she thought not. At last she decided to overcome her fear in the interests of education and better understanding. She would at least try to open their minds to modern truths. If she succeeded, good! If not, she was prepared to suffer the consequences.

In this spirit of patient martyrdom she waited for an opportunity to speak.

It came, surprisingly, one Saturday. Ordinarily that was a busy day at the Simpsons', a time for entertaining, so that Jade Snow was not free until too late to go anywhere, even had she had a place to go. But on this particular Saturday the Simpsons were away for the weekend, and by three in the afternoon Jade Snow was ready to leave the apartment with unplanned hours ahead of her. She didn't want to spend these rare hours of freedom in any usual way. And she didn't want to spend them alone.

"Shall I call Joe?"[1] she wondered. She had never telephoned to a boy before, and she debated whether it would be too forward. But she felt too happy and carefree to worry much, and she was confident that Joe would not misunderstand.

Even before reporting to mama that she was home, she ran downstairs to the telephone booth and gave the operator Joe's number. His mother answered and then went to call him while Jade Snow waited in embarrassment.

"Joe." She was suddenly tongue-tied. "Joe, I'm already home."

That wasn't at all what she wanted to say. What did she want to say?

"Hello! Hello!" Joe boomed back. "What's the matter with you! Are you all right?"

"Oh, yes, I'm fine. Only, only . . . well, I'm through working for the day." That was really all she had to say, but now it sounded rather pointless.

[1] JOE: an American boy several years older than Jade Snow.

"Isn't that wonderful? It must have been unexpected."
That was what was nice and different about Joe. He always
seemed to know without a lot of words. But because his
teasing was never far behind his understanding, he added
quickly, "I suppose you're going to study and go to bed
early."

Jade Snow was still not used to teasing and didn't know
how to take it. With an effort she swallowed her shyness
and disappointment. "I thought we might go for a walk . . .
that is, if you have nothing else to do . . . if you would care
to . . . if. . . ."

Joe laughed. "I'll go you one better. Suppose I take you
to a movie. I'll even get all dressed up for you, and you get
dressed up too."

Jade Snow was delighted. Her first movie with Joe! What
a wonderful day. In happy anticipation she put on her long
silk stockings, lipstick, and the nearest thing to a suit she
owned—a hand-me-down jacket and a brown skirt she had
made herself. Then with a bright ribbon tying back her
long black hair she was ready.

Daddy didn't miss a detail of the preparations as she
dashed from room to room. He waited until she was
finished before he demanded, "Jade Snow, where are you
going?"

"I am going out into the street," she answered.

"Did you ask my permission to go out into the street?"

"No, daddy."

"Do you have your mother's permission to go out into the
street?"

"No, daddy."

A sudden silence from the kitchen indicated that mama
was listening.

Daddy went on: "Where and when did you learn to be so
daring as to leave this house without permission of your
parents? You did not learn it under my roof."

It was all very familiar. Jade Snow waited, knowing that
daddy had not finished. In a moment he came to the point.

"And with whom are you going out into the street?"

It took all the courage Jade Snow could muster, remembering her new thinking, to say nothing. It was certain that

if she told daddy that she was going out with a boy whom
he did not know, without a chaperone, he would be convinced that she would lose her maidenly purity before the
evening was over.

"Very well," daddy said sharply. "If you will not tell me,
I forbid you to go! You are now too old to whip."

That was the moment.

Suppressing all anger, and in a manner that would have
done credit to her sociology instructor addressing his fresh-
man class, Jade Snow carefully turned on her mentally re-
hearsed speech.

"That is something you should think more about. Yes,
I am too old to whip. I am too old to be treated as a child.
I can now think for myself, and you and mama should not
demand unquestioning obedience from me. You should
understand me. There was a time in America when parents
raised children to make them work, but now the foreigners
regard them as individuals with rights of their own. I have
worked too, but now I am an individual besides being your
fifth daughter."

It was almost certain that daddy blinked, but after the
briefest pause he gathered himself together.

"Where," he demanded, "did you learn such an unfilial
theory?"

Mama had come quietly into the room and slipped into a
chair to listen.

"From my teacher," Jade Snow answered triumphantly,
"who you taught me is supreme after you, and whose judgment I am not to question."

Daddy was feeling pushed. Thoroughly aroused, he
shouted: "A little learning has gone to your head! How can
you permit a foreigner's theory to put aside the practical
experience of the Chinese, who for thousands of years have
preserved a most superior family pattern? Confucius had
already presented an organized philosophy of manners
and conduct when the foreigners were unappreciatively
persecuting Christ. Who brought you up? Who clothed
you, fed you, sheltered you, nursed you? Do you think you
were born aged sixteen? You owe honor to us before you
satisfy your personal whims."

Daddy thundered on, while Jade Snow kept silent.

"What would happen to the order of this household if each of you four children started to behave like individuals? Would we have one peaceful moment if your personal desires came before your duty? How could we maintain our self-respect if we, your parents, did not know where you were at night and with whom you were keeping company?"

With difficulty Jade Snow kept herself from being swayed by fear and the old familiar arguments. "You can be bad in the daytime as well as at night," she said defensively. "What could happen after eleven that couldn't happen before?"

Daddy was growing excited. "Do I have to justify my judgment to you? I do not want a daughter of mine to be known as one who walks the streets at night. Have you no thought for our reputations if not for your own? If you start going out with boys, no good man will want to ask you to be his wife. You just do not know as well as we do what is good for you."

Mama fanned daddy's wrath, "Never having been a mother, you cannot know how much grief it is to bring up a daughter. Of course we will not permit you to run the risk of corrupting your purity before marriage."

"Oh, mama!" Jade Snow retorted. "This is America, not China. Don't you think I have any judgment? How can you think I would go out with just any man?"

"Men!" daddy roared. "You don't know a thing about them. I tell you, you can't trust any of them."

Now it was Jade Snow who felt pushed. She delivered the balance of her declaration of independence: "Both of you should understand that I am growing up to be a woman in a society greatly different from the one you knew in China. You expect me to work my way through college— which would not have been possible in China. You expect me to exercise judgment in choosing my employers and my jobs and in spending my own money in the American world. Then why can't I choose my friends? Of course independence is not safe. But safety isn't the only consideration. You must give me the freedom to find some answers for myself."

Mama found her tongue first. "You think you are too good for us because you have a little foreign book knowledge."

"You will learn the error of your ways after it is too late," daddy added darkly.

By this Jade Snow knew that her parents had conceded defeat. Hoping to soften the blow, she tried to explain: "If I am to earn my living, I must learn how to get along with many kinds of people, with foreigners as well as Chinese. I intend to start finding out about them now. You must have confidence that I shall remain true to the spirit of your teachings. I shall bring back to you the new knowledge of whatever I learn."

Daddy and mama did not accept this offer graciously. "It is as useless for you to tell me such ideas as 'The wind blows across a deaf ear.' You have lost your sense of balance," daddy told her bluntly. "You are shameless. Your skin is yellow. Your features are forever Chinese. We are content with our proven ways. Do not try to force foreign ideas into my home. Go. You will one day tell us sorrowfully that you have been mistaken."

After that there was no further discussion of the matter. Jade Snow came and went without any questions being asked. In spite of her parents' dark predictions, her new freedom in the choice of companions did not result in a rush of undesirables. As a matter of fact, the boys she met at school were more concerned with copying her lecture notes than with anything else.

As for Joe, he remained someone to walk with and talk with. On the evening of Jade Snow's seventeenth birthday he took her up Telegraph Hill and gave her as a remembrance a sparkling grown-up bracelet with a card which read: "Here's to your making Phi Beta Kappa." And there under the stars he gently tilted her face and gave her her first kiss.

Standing straight and awkward in her full-skirted red cotton dress, Jade Snow was caught by surprise and without words. She felt that something should stir and crash within her, in the way books and the movies described, but nothing did. Could it be that she wasn't in lóve with Joe, in spite of liking and admiring him? After all, he was twenty-three and probably too old for her anyway.

Still she had been kissed at seventeen, which was cause for rejoicing. Laughing happily, they continued their walk.

But while the open rebellion gave Jade Snow a measure of freedom she had not had before, and an outer show of assurance, she was deeply troubled within. It had been simple to have daddy and mama tell her what was right and wrong; it was not simple to decide for herself. No matter how critical she was of them, she could not discard all they stood for and accept as a substitute the philosophy of the foreigners. It took very little thought to discover that the foreign philosophy also was subject to criticism, and that for her there had to be a middle way.

In particular, she could not reject the fatalism that was at the core of all Chinese thinking and behavior, the belief that the broad pattern of an individual's life was ordained by fate, although within that pattern he was capable of perfecting himself and accumulating a desirable store of good will. Should the individual not benefit by his good works, still the rewards would pass on to his children or his children's children. Epitomized by the proverbs "I save your life, for your grandson might save mine" and "Heaven does not forget to follow the path a good man walks," this was a fundamental philosophy of Chinese life which Jade Snow found fully as acceptable as some of the so-called scientific reasoning expounded in the sociology class, where heredity and environment were assigned all the responsibility for personal success or failure.

There was good to be gained from both concepts if she could extract and retain her own personally applicable com-bination. She studied her neighbor in class, Stella Green, for clues. Stella had grown up reading Robert Louis Steven-son, learning to swim and play tennis, developing a taste for roast beef, mashed potatoes, sweets, aspirin tablets, and soda pop, and she looked upon her mother and father as friends. But it was very unlikely that she knew where her great-grandfather was born, or whether or not she was related to another strange Green she might chance to meet. Jade Snow had grown up reading Confucius, learning to embroider and cook rice, developing a taste for steamed fish and bean sprouts, tea, and herbs, and she thought of her parents as people to be obeyed. She not only knew where her ancestors were born but where they were buried, and how many chickens and roast pigs should be brought annually to their graves to feast their spirits. She knew all of the branches of the Wong family, the relation of each to the other, and understood why daddy must help support the distant cousins in China who bore the sole responsibility of carrying on the family heritage by periodic visits to the burial grounds in Fragrant Mountains. She knew that one could purchase in a Chinese stationery store the printed record of her family tree relating their Wong line and other Wong lines back to the original Wong ancestors. In such a scheme the individual counted for little weighed against the family, and after sixteen years it was not easy to sever roots.

There were, alas, no books or advisers to guide Jade Snow in her search for balance between the pull from two cultures. If she chose neither to reject nor accept *in toto*,[2] she must sift both and make her decisions alone. It would not be an easy search. But pride and determination, which daddy had given her, prevented any thought of turning back. . . .

[2] *in toto:* completely.

FOR DISCUSSION

1. The author in 1938 was trying to arrive at a satisfactory combination of Chinese and American concepts about how a person should regard his life and his future. Was she looking for the impossible? Why, or why not?

2. How similar does the generation gap in this account seem to those you know of in American families of the 1970s?

Virginia Lee

b. 1923

Self-images which have been reinforced by generations of comforting inertia can retain a strong hold on a person's imagination, making him cling to them as true. And why not, if that is the way he finds his happiness?

In The House that Tai Ming Built, *Virginia Chin-lan Lee, whose family has lived in San Francisco for four generations, indulges herself in such comforting images. She describes the glory of a family dynasty, symbolized in an ancestral palace built by an early immigrant from the "Hills of Tong" (a euphemism for China), in loving, nostalgic terms, without the tension, the heartache, and the tragedy of mutilated families so matter-of-factly recounted in, for example, Betty Lee Sung's* Mountain of Gold. *And again, why not, if Virginia Lee is right in saying, "But that's how the Chinese in San Francisco's Chinatown really feel about their past"?*

The story of Tai Ming, who worked hard in California's gold fields to become an exemplar of the Chinese immigrant's dream of success, of Grandfather Kwong, with all his stereotyped quiet dignity and serenity of ancient China, and of Uncle Fook's sensitive love for the old arts of the Orient, has the charming, opium-pipe dream quality revealed in the following episode. Here is the old Chinese immigrant whose era may be long past, but whose existence once upon a time has left some indelible impressions on the minds of many survivors.

"Let me tell you about China the beautiful," we seem to hear Virginia Lee declare, "and let others unravel for you the long yarns of Chinese-American experience drenched in real tears."

Virginia Lee went to Chinese language schools until the eighth grade, studied Asian history in college, and married a man from South China. At present she is planning an Asian tour to gather material for her second book.

FROM
The House that Tai Ming Built

"Opium! Opium! as good as the immortal's pill; puff it but once and it is equal to entering heaven. . . ."

Grandfather Kwong was back in the Hills of Tong, and the little girl who had so desperately wanted to go with him to the House that Tai Ming Built had found a new companion. The words he had feebly uttered were meant as a farewell.

"Tomorrow I will come back again. May I come or may I not come?" Lin inquired of her elderly friend, who lay dreamily in the wooden bunk that occupied half of his small dingy room. Floating in heaven, he merely waved a thin yellow hand and nodded his shrunken head in consent. Lin dashed down the shaky, odorous, dark stairs, for the stories of demons and spirits which her old friend had told her were still fresh in her young head.

". . . and at the hour of the rat, the dogs howled and sleeping children suddenly screamed, for the eyes of dogs and children saw the evil spirit that we grown people only felt. . . ."

It was the next afternoon, and bearing a bag of fruit in her arms which she had taken in secret from home, Lin was once again with her old opium-smoking friend. ". . . It was the soul of a man who had died a violent death. He had returned to our village, wandering all about to find and steal a body, to reanimate it and continue to live. That night, huddled in my bed I felt the cold of a shaky form bend over and blow out the candle on the table near my bed I had left burning in fear of the dark. Then later the icy hand of the demon stroked my face, but right at that moment the village watchman on his route struck his gong, and instantly the demon disappeared. Early the next morning I took hammer and nails and built a wooden screen behind my door so that if the demon tried to enter my house again, he would bump his head and become confused. Then I changed the pathway leading to my door, for demons travel in a straight line, and in this way the evil spirit would be frustrated."

"Ah. . ." Lin sighed, knowing she surely would have a nightmare again that night.

"One morning in our village we found the body of a young farmer on the ground. His throat had been chewed to pieces. And do you know why? For years the woman he was married to had not been a woman but a were-tiger who had assumed the shape of a beautiful woman."

Lin, her coat draping her head and huddled shoulders, asked, "But how did you know it was a were-tiger?"

"Ah, Little One, all of us in the village searched for the dead man's wife, but in vain. Then we remembered how peculiar it was that such a beautiful woman had always shunned a mirror or a pool of water that might show her reflection; for you see, Little One, although a were-tiger has assumed the shape of a human, his true image is always reflected in a mirror."

Lin's friend climbed laboriously out of his wooden bunk and slowly walked to a kitchen table to pour two cups of tea. "Little One, enough of were-animals and evil spirits. Sit and partake of some tea. Ah . . . with a good companion and a cup of tea, one is equal to the immortals."

She liked the words and she repeated them, not understanding their meaning: "With a good companion and a cup of tea, one is equal to the immortals."

Her old friend's sharp black teeth clicked noisily together in joy at her appreciation of his words. His watery brown eyes were merry for a second, and he said in his feeble, trembling voice: "Little One, you like the proverbs? Ah, I know many more. Though I am but an old man now living in a shabby room, once I taught school in our village. Listen, Little One; I shall quote you more proverbs."

They sat facing each other on wooden stools, their elbows on the top of a stained red oilcloth covering a table littered with soft-bound books and stale food. Her friend sucked a slice of orange and Lin sucked a slice of orange. He took a sip of tea and she took a sip of tea. He began in his feeble, trembling voice, "The wise are happiest near water; the virtuous are happiest near hills."

She repeated it in his jingling fashion, stressing and prolonging the tones of the last word like the final upward stroke of a word character. "'The wise are happiest near water; the virtuous are happiest near hills.' Why, sir?"

His watery eyes twinkled for a second, and with a finger he wiped a teardrop away from his gaunt cheekbone.

"Because, Little One, the wise are active and restless like the waters; the virtuous are tranquil and firm like the solid mountains."

A sip of tea and a slice of orange again, and the wavering voice went on: "If you would enlarge your fields of happiness, you must level the soil in your heart." And like a proud teacher he pursed his withered mouth as Lin repeated the words she liked but did not understand.

"Little One, it means one must be honest and steady in all that one does."

One bony yellow finger poised in the air, eyes solemn, Lin's friend softly chanted, "He who tells me of my weakness is my teacher; he who tells me of my virtues does me harm." Then his finger tapped in rhythm to the words repeated out of her young mouth.

Then in a lively tempo he quoted one proverb after another, and just as rapidly Lin repeated each one. Though she was but six, her memory was precocious.

"As riches adorn the house, so virtue adorns the man.

"Return injury with justice, and return kindness with kindness.

"Be not distressed that men do not know you; be distressed that you do not know men."

The tempo became livelier still as he chanted and she repeated, "The superior man seeks to perfect the best in men; the mean man seeks to perfect the worst in men.

"The superior man is easy to serve and hard to please; the mean man is hard to serve and easy to please."

Suddenly the flapping sounds of wings beat against the little window directly above the bunk bed. Lin turned her head. A small gray pigeon perched on the window ledge, peeking in at them with wide-open eyes. Her old friend raised his head toward the window. He was not happy at the sight of the bird. With a bony hand and in a voice as loud as he could muster, he warned the pigeon, "Away! Away!"

The little pigeon tried to squeeze himself through the narrow slit of the opened window. Feverishly excited, his hands trembling, eyes rolling and lips quivering, Lin's old friend pressed a shaky hand on her shoulder to raise himself from his chair. Shoulders stooped, bony knees bent, toes pointed outward, he hopped on his worn slippers, his eyes every second on the pigeon. His thin hands clutched the soiled quilt, and with an effort he pulled himself up onto the bed. There he rested for a second in a kneeling position, then heaved a sigh, and stood up. Like a stern teacher of the old Confucian school, he pointed a warning finger at the pigeon, then pushed its beak away from the window. Finally, with a last convulsive effort, he shut the window, a highly visible cloud of dust mushrooming forth with the noise of the slam.

Solemnly, still standing on the bunk bed, he intoned, "If into your house flies the wild bird, misfortune will follow, mark my word!"

He remained standing on the bed until he was certain the pigeon had flown away. Again with much effort, he proceeded to come down. Standing close to Lin, he slapped his hands to get rid of the dust. Then with his head cocked, his withered mouth pursed, one hand on his hip, one finger on his forehead, he pondered upon the wisdom of what he had done as he said, "Perhaps I should have fried it for my supper."

He sat down. He said: "Little One, let us go on with the proverbs. Listen—the superior man is ruled by propriety; the mean man is ruled by law. The superior man thinks of righteousness; the mean man thinks of profit."

The sight of his hair in disarray disturbed Lin. The wind from the open window had blown it in all directions. Its disorder distracted her and caused her to stumble as she repeated the proverbs.

She said, "Sir, your hair is quite disordered. If you would give me a comb, I'll arrange your hair for you."

He said, "Little One, I don't have a comb." He lifted a thin hand to his mouth, moistened the palm generously, then put it to his head to slick his hair back to her satisfaction.

Lin's old friend laughed softly.

She asked, "What is so funny, sir?"

He said, "Little One, I don't have a comb; is that not unfortunate? Shall we then proceed to the Buddhist temple of our village to acquire one?"

She loved make-believe. She replied, "Yes, let's leave right now!"

Lin's old friend laughed in his weak, wavering voice. He said: "Little One! I have fooled you completely! Don't you know the favorite joke of us Sons of Tong? Little One, remember always that Buddhist monks shave their heads, and a Buddhist temple would be the least likely place to find a comb!"

Lin bounced up and down in her chair with laughter; surely Elder Brother would not be able to tell a more clever joke tonight at the evening rice!

A light rap on the table for silence and the wavering voice again:

"The superior man is satisfied and serene; the mean man is forever in anxiety.

"The superior man considers sincerity the most excellent of all virtues.

"The superior man is stern at a distance; mild up close; firm and clear in conversation."

Simultaneously they heaved deep sighs, rang out in joyous laughter, and sipped cool tea from chipped porcelain cups.

Lin's old friend spoke with deep conviction: "Little One, you are indeed a clever child!"

Said Lin with equal conviction, "Sir, you are indeed good of heart to say so!"

Said he, with palms outstretched, "Little One, we are so well acquainted; why then do you address me Sir this, Sir that?"

Said she, with palms outstretched, "Sir, it is always my mother who teaches me how to address my elders, and she is not here. How then do you wish me to address you, for I am most desirous of pleasing you?"

Her old friend chuckled softly. He said in his feeble voice, "So clever indeed! Little One, address me as uncle; that would be appropriate."

She nodded her small head in approval. She said, "Yes, uncle. Uncle, partake of some hot tea," and with a pair of unsteady small hands she poured tea for him out of a brown earthen teapot.

He began again, his hand holding one old ivory chopstick which he pointed in the air, "The superior man stands in awe of the laws of heaven; he stands in awe of all great men; he stands in awe of the wise words of the sages."

She commenced to repeat the words, but with a bony hand he silenced her as he continued, "The mean man, not knowing the laws of heaven, does not stand in awe of them; not understanding great men, does not respect them; not believing the words of wisdom, disparages them."

Preferring the superior man to the mean man, she repeated, "'The superior man stands in awe of the laws of heaven; he stands in awe of all great men; he stands in awe of the wise words of the sages.'"

"How clever indeed! A mind as good as the sages indeed! Let us see how clever you can be with this one.

Listen: The superior man is anxious that his eyes see clearly; anxious that his ears hear distinctly; anxious that his appearance be benevolent; anxious that his conduct be respectful; anxious that his speech be sincere; anxious that in business he is ethical; anxious when in doubt to question; anxious about difficulties when aroused; anxious about righteousness when tempted."

She drew a deep breath and recited rapidly, but halfway through she became confused and hung her head in shame.

"Ah, Little One, do not fret. Here, allow me to give you these books of proverbs. When you are a grown girl, you can read for yourself and learn."

Emulating the ways of her elders she refused, but he insisted. Then, after the lapse of a proper interval, she accepted the books with words of deepest gratitude. She hugged the books to her young breast and listened to her old friend.

"The superior man is anxious lest he should not get truth; he is not anxious that poverty is his lot."

His benevolence overwhelmed her young person, and seeing his shrunken, kind face, she remembered Grandfather Kwong, and her heart quickened with fear. Placing a small hand over his small bony hand, she asked, "Will you return to the Hills of Tong someday?"

He said, "Ah, to return to the Hills of Tong—that would be good. But, Little One, I have not the funds to return."

At this, in secret she was happy.

Lin's old friend got up from the wooden stool and walked over to a table near his bunk. Quietly she walked over and joined him and watched carefully as he took a small ivory stick to pick up a blob of opium from a tin. Then he held the stick over a gas jet flame, turning and turning it until the opium formed into a little round ball. Next he put the little ball of opium into the bowl of a long, slender pipe which he held in his bony hands with tender care. It was Lin's cue that she should make ready to leave. Very softly she walked out of the room after he uttered the words, "Opium, opium, as good as the immortal's pill. . . ."

"In autumn the trees shed their leaves; in spring they blossom again, but the cruelty of heaven is that when a man grows old, he cannot grow young again!"

Lin's old friend was unhappy as he talked, and Lin, with a gift of a single orange in her hand, was also unhappy. There were present in the room two white men, and she was concerned, for one orange would not be enough for the four of them.

"Uncle, what is the trouble? In all the many moons I have been to see you, I have never seen you like this."

He said: "Heaven has a path, but I did not tread it; hell has no door, but I charged into it. Little One, there can no longer be any more happy hours with us. Now you must learn the proverbs yourself. I have taught you the characters and you are clever; you will learn."

Her heart quickened. She said, "I do not understand! I do not understand! Why can there no longer be happy hours with us?"

His bony hands waved weakly in the air. "These two foreigners are going to take me somewhere for a few days. Then afterward I am returning to the Hills of Tong."

And although it had been almost a year since he had told her, she remembered and she cried out: "Uncle, you told me you had not the funds to return to the Hills of Tong!"

In sympathy he handed her a dirty handkerchief, and she wiped the tears from her young eyes. Patting her small hands, he said: "I am truly sorry; but, Little One, these two foreigners insist I return, and since they are so kind as to pay my passage fare, I must not offend them. Little One, is that not the way of the superior man?"

She nodded her unhappy head and replied in a choking voice, now fully understanding the words, "Yes—the superior man subdues himself; the mean man is resentful and domineering."

Lin's old friend walked slowly out of the room between the two white men. She stayed behind: there would be no more proverbs, no more stories of were-tigers and evil spirits, no more enchanting fables of the Eight Immortals. She ran out of the dingy room, and standing with legs apart and arms outstretched, she cried, as she had cried to Grandfather Kwong, "Uncle, take me with you to the Hills of Tong." But he did not hear her, and with his soiled handkerchief pressed to her sobbing mouth, she watched him disappear.

Years later she came upon the old books her opium-addict friend had given her. Opening them, she remembered his feeble, trembling voice, his withered finger poised in the air as he quoted: "He who tells me of my weakness is my teacher; he who tells me of my virtues does me harm." Putting the books aside, she knew then what as a little heartbroken girl she did not know: that last day her old friend had been taken away by narcotics agents to be deported back to the Hills of Tong.

FOR DISCUSSION

1. "The wisest are happiest near water; the virtuous are happiest near hills." What does this proverb tell you about certain Chinese concepts relating to man and nature?

2. What are the realistic elements and what are the fairy-tale elements in the story?

Frank
Chin

b. 1940

Asked about the one thing he most wishes his audience to perceive through his writing, Frank Chin replied: "The sensibility, the kind of sensibility that is neither Chinese of China nor white-American. The sensibility derived from the peculiar experience of a Chinese born in this country [Berkeley, California] some thirty years ago, with all the stigmas attached to his race, but felt by himself alone as an individual human being."

Frank Chin sees himself in a unique position to transmit the truly identifiable Chinese-American experience because he is young enough to see through the stereotyped images with which many Chinese in America above the age of forty identify themselves, and yet he is old enough to remember what it was like to be a Chinese in the United States during World War II. As to the Chinese of the postwar era, in Frank's view their Chineseness is being rapidly absorbed by the white-American values. And those young Chinese, either championing the cause of, or resisting the emergence of, a new China, are so busy fighting on the active front of politics that they unavoidably fall short of being fully sensitive to all the subtle pressures and forces operating on each individual.

To start building a repository of materials on the Chinese-American experience, free-lance writer Frank is working with several friends to transcribe taped interviews with representative Chinese in West Coast communities from Seattle to San Diego. After that will come a novel featuring a number of Chinese characters whom he discovered during his interviews. His novelette "Goong Hai Fot Choy" has been included in Nineteen Necromancers from Now *(Doubleday, 1970), edited by Ishmael Reed.*

"Food for All His Dead" was first published in the journal Contact. *The title refers to the traditional Chinese practice of offering food to the dead on anniversaries and other festive occasions throughout the year, but in making such a reference, the author is suggesting that the old tradition of China really means nothing to the Chinese-Americans born in Chinatown, and that it is foolish to assume otherwise. The setting of the story is the forty-fifth anniversary of the founding of the Republic of China, and on such an occasion San Francisco's Chinatown stages a gala celebration, complete with lion and dragon dances and a festooned stage where everybody who is somebody in that Chinese community gets either to make a speech or to sit being watched and admired.*

While studying at the University of California at Berkeley, Frank Chin edited the undergraduate humor magazine, The Pelican. *Later he attended the State University of Iowa. For a while he taught at San Francisco State College and wrote film reviews in Hollywood. At present he is traveling with his typewriter in the western United States, generally making San Francisco his base camp.*

Food for All His Dead

"Jus' forty-fie year 'go, Doctah Sun Yat-sen free China from da Manchus. Dats' why all us Chinee, alla ovah da woil, are celebrate Octob' tan or da Doubloo Tan . . . !"

The shouted voice came through the open bathroom window. The shouting and music was still loud after rising through the night's dry air; white moths jumped on the air, danced through the window over the voice, and lighted quickly on the wet sink, newly reddened from his father's

attack. Johnny's arms were around his father's belly, holding the man upright against the edge of the sink to keep the
man's mouth high enough to spit lung blood into the
drain. . . .

The man's belly shrank and filled against Johnny's arms
as the man breathed and spat, breathed and spat, the belly
shrinking and filling. The breaths and bodies against each
other shook with horrible rhythms that could not be
numbed out of Johnny's mind. "Pride," Johnny thought,
"pa's pride for his reputation for doing things . . . except
dying. He's not proud of dying, so it's a secret between
father and son. . . ." At the beginning of the man's death,
when he had been Johnny's father, still commanding and
large, saying, "Help me. I'm dying; don't tell," and remov-
ing his jacket and walking to the bathroom. Then came the
grin—pressed lips twisted up into the cheeks—hiding the
gathering blood and drool. Johnny had cried then, knowing
his father would die. But now the man seemed to have
been always dying and Johnny always waiting, waiting
with what he felt was a coward's loyalty to the dying, for
he helped the man hide his bleeding and was sick himself,
knowing he was not waiting for the man to die but waiting
for the time after death when he could relax.

"*. . . free from da yoke of Manchu slab'ry, in'epen'ence,
no moah queue[1] on da head! Da's wha'fo' dis big a parade!
An' here, in San Francisco, alla us Chinee-'mellican 're
pwowd! . . .*"

"It's all gone . . . I can't spit any more. Get my shirt, boy.
I'm going to make a speech tonight. . . ." The man slipped
from the arms of the boy and sat on the toilet lid and closed
his mouth. His bare chest shone as if washed with dirty
cooking oil and looked as if he should have been chilled,
not sweating, among the cold porcelain and tile of the bathroom.

To the sound of herded drums and cymbals, Johnny
wiped the sweat from his father's soft body and dressed

[1] *queue* (kyo͞o): pigtail.

him without speaking. He was full of the heat of wanting to cry for his father but would not.

His father was heavier outside the house.

They staggered each other across the alleyway to the edge of Portsmouth Square. They stood together at the top of the slight hill, their feet just off the concrete onto the melted fishbone grass, and could see the brightly lit reviewing stand, and they saw over the heads of the crowd, the dark crowd of people standing in puddles of each other, moving like oily things and bugs floating on a tide; to their left, under trees, children played and shouted on swings and slides; some ran toward Johnny and his father and crouched behind their legs to hide from giggling girls. And they could see the street and the parade beyond the crowd. The man stood away from the boy but held tightly to Johnny's arm. The man swallowed a greasy sound and grinned. "I almost feel I'm not dying now. Parades are like that. I used to dance the Lion Dance in China, boy. I was always in the parades."

Johnny glanced at his father and saw the man's eyes staring wide with the skin around the eyes stretching for the eyes to open wider, and Johnny patted his father's shoulder and watched the shadows of children running across the white sand of the play area. He was afraid of watching his father die here; the man was no longer like his father or a man; perhaps it was the parade. But the waiting, the lies and waiting so long with a flesh going to death that the person was no longer real as a life but a parody of live things, grinning. The man was a fish drying and shrinking inside its skin on the sand, crazy, mimicking swimming, Johnny thought, but a fish could be lifted and slapped against a stone, thrown to cats; for his father, Johnny could only wait and help the man stay alive without helping him die. "That's probably where you got the disease," Johnny said.

"Where, boy?"

"Back in China."

"No, I got it here. I was never sick for one day in China." The man began walking down the hill toward the crowd. "Back in China. . . ."

They walked down the hill, the man's legs falling into steps with his body jerking after his falling legs; Johnny held his father, held the man back to keep him from falling over his own feet. The man's breath chanted dry and powdered out of his mouth and nostrils to the rhythm of the drums, and his eyes stared far ahead into the parade; his lips opened and showed brick-colored teeth in his grin. "Not so fast, *ah-bah!*" Johnny shouted and pulled at his father's arm. He was always frightened at the man's surges of nervous life.

"Don't run," Johnny said, feeling his father's muscles stretch as he pulled Johnny down the hill toward the crowd. "Stop running, pa!" And his father was running and breathing out fog into the hot night and sweating dirty oil, and trembling his fleshy rump inside his baggy trousers, dancing in stumbles with dead senses. "Pa, not so fast, dammit! You're going to have another attack! Slow down!"

"I can't stop, boy."

They were in the shadow of the crowd now, and children chased around them.

"Look! There they are!" the man said.

"Dere you're, ladies and genullmans! Eben da lion are bow in respack to us tonigh'!"

The crowd clapped and whistled, and boys shoved forward to see. Old women, roundbacked in their black overcoats, lifted their heads to smile; they stood together and nodded, looking like clumps of huge beetles with white faces.

"Closer to the platform, boy; that's where I belong," the man said. He leaned against Johnny's shoulder and coughed out of his nostrils. Johnny heard the man swallow and cringed. The man was grinning again, his eyes anxious, the small orbs jumping scared spiders all over the sockets. "Aren't you happy you came, boy? Look at all the people."

"Take time to catch your breath, *ah-bah*. Don't talk. It's wrong for you to be here anyhow."

"Nothing's wrong, boy; don't you see all your people happy tonight? As long as . . ." he swallowed and put his head against Johnny's cheek, then made a sound something like laughter, "as I've been here . . . do you understand my Chinese?" Then slowly in English, catching quick breaths between his words, "I be here, allabody say dere chillren're gonna leab Chinatong and go way, but 'snot so, huh?" His voice was low, a guttural monotone. "Look a'em all; dey still be Chinee. I taught da feller dat teach dem to dance how to do dat dancer boy. Johnny? dis're you home, here, an' I know you gat tire, but alla you fran's here, an' dey likee you." His face was speaking close to Johnny and chilled the boy's face with hot breath.

The boy did not look at his father talking to him but, stared stiffly out to the street, watching the glistening arms of boys jerking the bamboo skeletons of silk-hided lions over their heads. His father was trying to save him again, Johnny thought, trying to be close like he had been to him how long ago when his father was a hero from the war. The man spoke as if he had saved his life to talk to his son now, tonight, here among the eyes and sounds of Chinese.

"I'm sorry, *ah-bah*, I can't help it . . ." was all Johnny could answer sincerely. He knew it would be cruel to say, "Pa, I don't want to be a curiosity like the rest of the Chinese here. I want to be something by myself," so he did not, not only because of the old man, but because he was not certain he believed himself; it had been easy to believe his own shouted words when he was younger and safe with his parents; it had been easy not to like what he had then—when he knew he could stay; then, when the man was fat and not dying, they were separate and could argue, but not now; now he was favored with the man's secret; they were horribly bound together now. The old man was dying and still believing in the old ways, still sure—even brave, perhaps—and that meant something to Johnny.

"An' you see dam bow in respack now, an' da's good lucks to ev'eybody!"

The lion dancers passed, followed by a red convertible with boys beating a huge drum on the back seat.

Johnny knew the parades; the lion dancers led the wait for the coming of the long dragon, and the end. The ends of the parades with the dragon were the most exciting, were the loudest moment before the chase down the streets to keep the dragon in sight. He was half aware of the air becoming brittle with the noise of the dances and the crowd, and, with his father now, was almost happy, almost anxious, dull, the way he felt when he was tired and staring in a mirror, slowly realizing that he was looking at his own personal reflection; he felt pleased and depressed, as if he had just prayed for something.

"You know," the man said, "I wan' you to be somebody here. Be doctor, mak' moneys and halp da Chinee, or lawyer, or edgenerer, make moneys and halp, and people're respack you." He patted the boy's chest. "You tall me now you won' leab here when I die, hokay?"

"I don't know, pa." The boy looked down to the trampled grass between his feet and shrugged off what he did not want to say. They were hopeless to each other now. He looked over his shoulder to his father and could not answer the chilled face, and they stared a close moment onto each other and were private, holding each other and waiting.

Policemen on motorcycles moved close to the feet of the crowd to move them back. The boys wearing black-and-red silk trousers and white sweatshirts, coaxing the clumsy dragon forward with bells and shafts, could be seen now; they were dancing and shouting past the reviewing stand. The dragon's glowing head lurched side to side, rose and fell, its jaw dangling after the goading boys. As the dragon writhed and twisted about itself, boys jumped in and out from under its head and belly to keep the dragon fresh.

"Maybe I'm not Chinese, pa! Maybe I'm just a Chinese accident. You're the only one that seems to care that I'm Chinese." The man glared at the boy and did not listen. "Pa, most of the people I don't like are Chinese. They even *laugh* with accents, Christ!" He turned his head from the man, sorry for what he said. It was too late to apologize.

"You dare to talk to your father like that?" the man shouted in Chinese. He stood back from the boy, raised himself and slapped him, whining through his teeth as his arm swung heavily toward the boy's cheek. "You're no son of mine! No son! I'm ashamed of you!"

The shape of the bamboo skeleton was a shadow within the thinly painted silk of the dragon, and boys were shouting inside.

"Pa, *ah-bah*, I'm sorry."

"Get me up to the platform; I gotta make a speech."

"Pa, you've got to go home."

"I'm not dead yet; you'll do as I say."

"All right, I'll help you up because you won't let me help you home. But I'll leave you up there, pa. I'll leave you for ma and sister to bring home."

"From da Pres'den, of da United State' 'mellica! 'To alla ob da Chinee-'mellican on da celebrate ob dere liberate from da Manchu....'"

"I'm trying to make you go home for your own good."

"You're trying to kill me with disgrace. All right, leave me. Get out of my house, too."

"Pa, I'm trying to help you. You're dying!" The boy reached for his father, but the man stepped away. "You'll kill ma by not letting her take care of you."

"Your mother's up on the platform waiting for me."

"Because she doesn't know how bad you are. I do. I have a right to make you go home."

"It's my home, not yours. Leave me alone." The man walked the few steps to the edge of the platform and called his wife. She came down and helped him up. She glanced out but did not see Johnny in the crowd. Her cheeks were made up very pink and her lipstick was still fresh; she looked very young next to Johnny's father, but her hands were old, and seemed older because of the bright nail polish and jade bracelet.

Johnny knew what his father would tell his mother and knew he would have to trust them to be happy without him. Perhaps he meant he would have to trust himself to be happy without them ... the feeling would pass; he would

wait and apologize to them both, and he would not have to
leave, perhaps. Everything seemed wrong, all wrong, yet
everyone, in his own way, was right. He turned quickly and
walked out of the crowd to the children's play area. He sat
on a bench and stretched his legs straight out in front of
him. The dark old women in black coats stood by on the
edges of the play area watching the nightbleached faces of
children flash in and out of the light as they ran through
each other's shadows. Above him, Johnny could hear the
sound of pigeons in the trees. Chinatown was the same and
he hated it now. Before, when he was younger, and went
shopping with his mother, he had enjoyed the smells of the
shops and seeing colored toys between the legs of walking
people; he had been proud to look up and see his mother
staring at the numbers on the scales that weighed meat, to
see the shopkeepers smile and nod at her. And at night, he
had played here, like the children chasing each other in
front of him now.

"What'sa wrong, Johnny? Tire?" He had not seen the
girl standing in front of him. He sat up straight and smiled.
"You draw more pitchers on napkin for me tonigh'?"

"No, I was with pa." He shrugged. "You still got the
napkins, huh?"

"I tole you I want dem. I'm keeping 'em." She wore a
short white coat over her red *cheongsam,* and her hair
shook down over her face from the wind.

"I wanta walk," he said. "You wanta walk?"

"I gotta gat home before twalve."

"Me too."

"I'll walk for you dan, okay?" She smiled and reached a
hand down for him.

"You'll walk *with* me, not *for* me. You're not a dog." He
stood and took her hand. He enjoyed the girl; she listened
to him; he did not care if she understood what he said or
knew what he wanted to say. She listened to him, would
listen with her eyes staring with a wide frog's stare until
he stopped speaking, then her body would raise and she
would sigh a curl of girl's voice and say, "You talk so
nice. . . ."

The tail of an embroidered dragon showed under her white coat and seemed to sway as her thigh moved. "You didn' come take me to the parade, Johnny?"

"I was with pa." Johnny smiled. The girl's hand was dryfeeling, cold and dry like a skin of tissue-paper-covered flesh. They walked slowly, rocking forward and back as they stepped up the hill. "I'm always with pa, huh?" he said bitterly. "I'm sorry."

"'sall right. Is he still dying?"

"Everyone's dying here; it's called the American's common cold."

"Don' talk you colleger stuff to me! I don' unnerstan' it, Johnny."

"He's still dying . . . always. I mean, sometimes I think he won't die or is lying and isn't dying."

"Wou'n't that be good, if he weren't dying? And if it was all a joke? You could all laugh after."

"I don't know, Sharon!" He whined on the girl's name and loosened her hand, but she held.

"Johnny?"

"Yeah?"

"What'll you do if he dies?"

Johnny did not look at the girl as he answered, but lifted his head to glance at the street full of lights and people walking between moving cars. Grant Avenue. He could smell incense and caged squabs, the dank smell of damp fish heaped on tile from the shops now. "I think I'd leave. I know what that sounds like, like I'm waiting for him to die so I can leave; maybe it's so. Sometimes I think I'd kill him to stop all this waiting and lifting him to the sink and keeping it a secret. But I won't do that."

"You won' do that. . ." Sharon said.

"An' now, I like to presan' da Pres'den ob da Chinee Benabolen'. . . ."

"My father," Johnny said.

The girl clapped her hands over her ears to keep her hair from jumping in the wind. "You father?" she said.

"I don't think so," Johnny said. They walked close to the walls, stepped almost into doorways to allow crowding people to pass them going down the hill toward the voice. They smelled grease and urine of open hallways, and heard music like birds being strangled as they walked over iron gratings.

"You don't think so what?" Sharon asked, pulling him toward the crowd.

"I don't think so what you said you didn't think so. . . ." He giggled, "I'm sort of funny tonight. I was up all last night listening to my father practice his speech in the toilet and helping him bleed when he got mad. And this morning I started to go to classes and fell asleep on the bus; so I didn't go to classes, and I'm still awake. I'm not tired but kind of stupid with no sleep, dig, Sharon?"

The girl smiled and said, "I dig, Johnny. You the same way every time I see you almos'.'"

"And I hear myself talking all this stupid stuff, but it's sort of great, you know? Because I have to listen to what I'm saying or I'll miss it."

"My mother say you cute."

They were near the top of the street now, standing in front of a wall stand with a fold-down shelf covered with Chinese magazines, nickel comic books, postcards, and Japanese souvenirs of Chinatown. Johnny, feeling ridiculous with air between his joints and his cheeks tingling with the anxious motion of the crowd, realized he was tired, then realized he was staring at the boy sitting at the wall stand and staring at the boy's leather cap.

"What are you loo' at, huh?" the boy said in a girl's voice. Sharon pulled at Johnny and giggled. Johnny giggled and relaxed to feeling drunk and said, "Are you really Chinese?"

"What're you ting, I'm a Negro soy sauce chicken?"

"Don't you know there's no such thing as a real Chinaman in all of America? That all we are are American Indians cashing in on a fad?"

"Fad? Don' call me fad. You fad youselv.'"

"No, you're not Chinese, don't you understand? You see it all started when a bunch of Indians wanted to quit being Indians and fighting the cavalry and all, so they left the reservation, see?"

"In'ian?"

"And they saw that there was this big kick about China-men, so they braided their hair into queues and opened up laundries and restaurants and started reading Margaret Mead and Confucius and Pearl Buck and became respect-able Chinamen and gained some self-respect."

"Chinamong! You battah not say Chinamong."

"But the reservation instinct stuck, years of tradition, you see? Something about needing more than one Indian to pull off a good rain dance or something, so they made Chinatown! And here we are!"

He glanced around him and grinned. Sharon was laugh-ing, her shoulders hopping up and down. The boy blinked, then pulled his cap lower over his eyes. "It's all right to come out now, you see?" Johnny said. "Indians are back in vogue and the Chinese kick is wearing out. . . ." He laughed until he saw the boy's confused face. "Aww nuts," he said, "this is no fun."

He walked after Sharon through the crowd, not feeling the shoulders and women's hips knocking against him. "I'd like to get outta here so quick, Sharon; I wish I had something to do! What do I do here? What does anybody do here? I'm bored! My mother's a respected woman because she can tell how much monosodium glutamate is in a dish by smelling it, and because she knows how to use a spit-toon in a restaurant. Everybody's Chinese here, Sharon."

"Sure!" the girl laughed and hopped to kiss his cheek. "Didn' you like that?"

"Sure, I liked it, but I'm explaining something. You know, nobody shoulda let me grow up and go to any school outside of Chinatown." They walked slowly, twisting to allow swaggering men to pass. "Then, maybe everything would be all right now, you see? I'm stupid, I don't know what I'm talking about. I shouldn't go to parades and see all those kids. I remember when I was a kid. Man, then I knew everything. I knew all my aunts were beautiful, and all my cousins were small, and all my uncles were heroes from the war and the strongest guys in the world that smoked cigars and swore, and my grandmother was a queen of women." He nodded to himself. "I really had it made then, really, and I knew more then than I do now."

"What'd'ya mean? You smart now! You didn't know how to coun' or spall, or nothin'; now you in colleger."

"I had something then, you know? I didn't have to ask about anything; it was all there; I didn't have questions; I knew who I was responsible to, who I should love, who I was afraid of, and all my dogs were smart."

"You lucky, you had a dog!" The girl smiled.

"And all the girls wanted to be nurses; it was fine! Now, I'm just what a kid should be—stupid, embarrassed. I don't know who can tell me anything.

"Here, in Chinatown, I'm undoubtedly the most enlightened, the smartest fortune cookie ever baked to a golden brown, but out there . . . God!" He pointed down to the end of Grant Avenue, past ornamented lamps of Chinatown to the tall buildings of San Francisco, "Here, I'm fine—and bored stiff. Out there—Oh, hell, what'm I talking about. You don't know either; I try to tell my father, and he doesn't know, and he's smarter'n you."

"If you don't like stupids, why'd you talk to me so much?"

"Because I like you. You're the only thing I know that doesn't fight me. . . . You know I think I've scared myself into liking this place for a while. See what you've done by walking with me? You've made me a good Chinese for my parents again. I think I'll sell firecrackers." He was dizzy now, overwhelmed by the sound of too many feet and clicking lights. "I even like you, Sharon!" He swung her arm and threw her ahead of him and heard her laugh. "My grandmother didn't read English until she watched television and read 'The End'; that's pretty funny, what a kick!" They laughed at each other and ran among the shoulders of the crowd, shouting "Congratulations!" in Chinese into the shops, "Congratulations!" to a bald man with long hair growing down the edges of his head.

"Johnny, stop! You hurt my wrist!"

It was an innocent kiss in her hallway, her eyes closed

so tight the lashes shrank and twitched like insect legs, and her lips puckered long, a dry kiss with closed lips. "Good night, Johnny . . . John," she said. And he waved and watched her standing in the hallway, disappearing as he walked down the stairs; then, out of sight, he ran home.

He opened the door to the apartment and hoped that his father had forgotten. "Fine speech, pa!" he shouted.

His little sister came out of her room, walking on the toes of her long pajamas. "Brother? Brother, *ah-bah*, he's sick!" she said. She looked straight up to Johnny as she spoke and nodded. Johnny stepped past his sister and ran to the bathroom and opened the door. His mother was holding the man up to the sink with one hand and holding his head with the other. The man's mess spattered over her *cheongsam*. The room, the man, everything, was uglier because of his mother's misery in her bright *cheongsam*. "*Ah-bah?*" Johnny said gently as if calling the man from sleep for dinner. They did not turn. He stepped up behind the woman. "I can do that, *ah-mah;* I'm a little stronger than you."

"Don't you touch him! You!" She spoke with her cheek against the man's back and her eyes closed. "He told me what you did, what you said, and you're killing him! If you want to leave, just go! Stop killing this man!"

"Not me, ma. He's been like this a long time. I've been helping him almost every night. He told me not to tell you."

"You think I don't know? I've seen you in here with him when I wanted to use the bathroom at night, and I've crept back to bed without saying anything because I know your father's pride. And you want to go and break it in a single night! First it's your telling everybody how good you are! Now go and murder your father. . . ."

"Ma, I'm sorry. He asked me, and I tried to make him understand. What do you want me to do, lie? I'll call a doctor."

"Get out; you said you're going to leave, so get out," the man said, lifting his head.

"I'll stay, ma, *ah-bah*, I'll stay."

"It's too late," his mother said. "I don't want you here."

The time was wrong . . . nobody's fault that his father was dying; perhaps, if his father was not dying out of his mouth, Johnny could have argued and left or stayed, but now, he could not stay without hate. "Ma,. I said I'm calling a doctor. . . ."

After the doctor came, Johnny went to his room and cried loudly, pulling the sheets from his bed and kicking at the wall until his foot became numb. He shouted his hate for his father and ignorant mother into his pillow until his face was wet with tears. His sister stood next to his bed and watched him, patting his ankle and saying over and over, "Brother, don't cry, brother. . . ."

Johnny sat up and held the small girl against him. "Be a good girl," he said. "You're going to have my big room now. I'm moving across the bay to school." He spoke very quietly to his sister against the sound of their father's spitting.

Sharon held his sister's elbow and marched behind Johnny and his mother. A band played in front of the coffin, and over the coffin was a large photograph of the dead man. Johnny had a miniature of the photograph in his wallet and would always carry it there. Without being told, he had dressed and was marching now beside his mother behind the coffin and the smell of sweet flowers. It was a parade of black coats and hats, and they all wore sunglasses against the sun; the sky was green, seen through the glasses, and the boys playing in Portsmouth Square had green shadows about them. A few people stopped on the street and watched.

FOR DISCUSSION

1. What made the older man proud of his Chinatown environment? What made his son feel unhappy there?

2. Why did Johnny say that there were no real Chinamen?

3. How effective is the dialect the author uses to characterize certain persons in the story? Does it make them sound real, or just funny?

Diana
Chang

b. 1934

The setting of Diana Chang's novel The Frontiers of Love
*is the last days of the Japanese occupation of Shanghai,
and the principal character, Sylvia Chen, is Eurasian.
Her world is different from that of Jade Snow Wong or
Pardee Lowe, and there in the tense situation of Shanghai's International Settlement, Sylvia, caught in the
conflict between her American mother and her other relatives, who are Chinese, struggles toward a consistent
personal identity. Two other main characters are also
Eurasians—one of them pursues love in all its emotional
and sensual intensity; the other, tortured by his background, seeks wholeness by losing himself in the larger
issue of communism.*

*Diana Chang was born in New York of a Chinese father
and a Eurasian mother. She lived in Peiping, Nanking, and
Shanghai until the end of World War II, returning to the
United States to be graduated from Barnard College in
1955. Besides* The Frontiers of Love, *she has three other
novels* (A Woman of Thirty, A Passion for Life, The Only
Game in Town) *and many published poems to her credit.
She is also an editor of* The American Pen, *a quarterly of
the P.E.N. Club, an international writers' association.*

FROM
The Frontiers of Love

The night before, Sylvia Chen had dreamed heavily, and awakened reluctantly in the morning. Later that day, she thought, she would probably have proof again that her dreams were often reversed in time—they did not always come after the event which might have caused them but often before, as though they were forecasts of the weather ahead.

"Come in," Sylvia said a few hours after waking, and as she said it, it sounded familiar, a cue that would lead her forward into that Saturday, and illuminate what she had dreamed. Though she had not heard a sound, she knew her father was standing by the door of her room. His hesitancy could reach her no matter how occupied she was; it traveled along her nerves and stammered in her senses.

"Come in, do," she insisted, but ungenerously did not turn around from her book.

The afternoon had just begun, taking the city in its lap. Her father now stood at her window, looking over the wall that hedged in the open garden of their neighbor's property. He cleared his throat, and she could see him leaning on the sill, turning his head to the right where another apartment house, a duplicate of their own, stood casting its shadow into their courtyard. The Chinese families who lived there took long siestas on the narrow balconies. Only the servants moved around below, soundlessly, in white jackets and black trousers, straightening the wash or taking in the deliveries. To Sylvia the after-lunch quiet seemed to give the scene the quality of a fable. Beyond, on the near horizon, the intersection of streets was quiet. Bicycles, rickshaws, and pedestrians moved slowly in the simmering heat.

She could feel her father struggling within himself to speak, to appeal to her. Stubbornly, she did not want to help him.

"Sylvia," he brought out at last, almost plaintively and without looking at her, "your mother is mad at me."

She turned to stare at the back of his head, forcing her eyes to be noncommittal. It always shocked her to hear him utter in his Chinese accent such colloquial phrases as "mad at me" or "sore at them." He had a long face for a Chinese and a high, receding forehead; these expressions were wholly out of keeping with this fine and tailored face, and his rather remote air.

"But that's not so serious, is it?" Sylvia asked, and regretted her tone immediately. He had often confessed to her that before his children he felt half-relic, half-contemporary. Of course, he often pointed out, children were one's equals in modern China, but today she felt he was prepared to reverse that—he was almost equal to his daughter.

"Couldn't you—couldn't you just go in and say a word to her?" he asked. He turned around, smiling; his smile always grew in proportion to his distress. "It's so much easier for you, you see."

She knew he would let himself say no more. His strict code of dignity would not allow it, and already she was beginning to yield, to do his bidding, as she always did, for no one but her mother could stand up to his soft insistence. Because he so feared direct encounters, Sylvia had never dared to question anything he did or said. Even to have remarked, "But I think it is wrong for me to arbitrate every time," would have seemed a frontal attack on his delicate ego. They were prisoners of their shyness with each other.

But Sylvia couldn't resist saying in a grudging tone, "But of course, for this is the land of the go-between," and as an unwilling one, got up and walked into the living room. A barricade of static hung between it and the bedroom where Helen, her mother, was sitting. She was probably traveling around the world on the impetus of her anger.

"Mother," Sylvia ordered, as soon as she reached the bedroom door. "Mother, stop sulking at once!"

Helen looked up from her nails, which she was filing by the open window. Sylvia could see her blue-eyed stare in the mirror. Her back was turned to her, like a cat's, deaf to everything except her own willfulness.

"Helen Ames Chen," she cajoled, for with her mother Sylvia was not at all shy. "Mother," she said again, but only halfheartedly. Her parents' quarrels were like beds that had to be made up every morning, only to be disordered again. In the end, Liyi would come into the bedroom, feeling that the situation had been changed by his daughter's ineffectual words, and Helen would shed a few tears, and they would seem to rediscover each other. They would seem bride and groom again. Helen might go into peals of senseless laughter, and Liyi would stand beside her, plaiting her long blonde hair, proud and pleased as a new husband.

"Oh, for pity's sake, mother!" Sylvia said, for Helen refused to respond. Her mock wail made her sound adolescent to herself. At home, she thought, as she stood in the doorway, not knowing what to do next, you had to discount five years from your age. At home, no child could act adult without feeling he was disinheriting his parents. They made you feel guilty that years affected you at all. Relationships were like pressures that pushed you in thirty-six directions of the compass. But, as in a crowded streetcar, if you learned how to maintain your balance against all the weights, you might arrive at yourself.

"Mother," Sylvia said with a sigh, feeling her father moving nervously in the living room. "Let's go for a walk, mother. Just you and I, and we'll splurge and have ice cream somewhere. Just like sisters."

Helen stirred at that, as easily mollified and distracted as a child, and before she could make a show of reluctance, Sylvia continued, "I'll get dressed and be right back," and left. Out of the corner of her eye, she caught her father's delighted wink. But she did not acknowledge it. Each of her parents had a way of wanting to make her an accomplice. . . .

No one, Sylvia thought, could do anything more out-
rageous in Shanghai than take a walk on Bubbling Well
Road in the International Settlement and have ice cream.
The ice cream was an anachronism in the mouth, sliding
down like a memory from her tongue to her stomach, as
she let the cream and the luxury absorb her. There wasn't
much ice cream in Shanghai these days; only infants and
the very ill were able to get rations of milk, for the Japanese
had killed most of the cows at the beginning of the war.
Sylvia could see rows of brown, white, and speckled cows
standing in the fields and dairies, standing at ease on three
legs and munching, waiting to be machine-gunned by the
conquerors to provide meat for their troops.

Sylvia looked at her mother now with new eyes—famil-
iarity had an unfortunate way of breeding a perspicacity
which almost denied a mother an independent identity.
As though the sparkling light of the afternoon illuminated
Helen, Sylvia had a strange sense of "remembering" her
against the background of Shanghai, a city barricaded for
so long. Americans like her mother had been allowed to
stay out of the internment camps because of their Chinese
husbands; instead they were required to wear red arm
bands with numbers printed on them. She was conspic-
uous—as Sylvia had always found her mother conspic-
uous—and to any Japanese gendarme[1] who wanted to stop her
and inspect her identity card, Helen was number 123.

They continued down the avenue, while Helen said,
"Now if we were back in New York," but Sylvia was not
listening. . . .

"Now if we were back in New York," Helen repeated
and went on, "we could take in a Broadway show or spend
a weekend in Connecticut. We could go up to the Cloisters,
or the Frick Museum, have dinner in the Tavern on the
Green, and then take a long, long drive on those highways
they have in America. You remember them, dear. You must
remember the traffic and the signs everywhere, the small
towns and wayside places, busy gas stations and certified

---

[1] GENDARME (zhän'därm): French for "police officer."

rest rooms." Sylvia's breath caught slightly as she looked
at her mother striding purposefully down the sidewalk,
making a bit of Philadelphia here in Shanghai because of
her sturdy oxfords and the aggressive swing of her legs.
Mother was homesick. Helen was homesick for America,
and Sylvia felt green and tender for her.

"I'm so sorry," Sylvia said, for her mother was very far
from home.

"Are you really?" Helen asked sharply, for she could
not sustain dreaminess for long. "Sorry because we ever
came back? But you wanted to." It was true; Sylvia had
hated America that year. "Sorry because out here we're
just decaying, out here in the middle of nowhere." "Out
here" was the vocabulary of extraterritoriality[2] and colo-
nialism, and Helen meant it literally, in the Rudyard Kip-
ling sense, white man's burden and all. Out here in the
jungle, out here in the desert, out here among the savages,
out here in the leper colony. And the Chinese to her were
part savage, part leprous, and totally mysterious.

But it's natural for her to think this way, Sylvia reminded
herself, tamping down the pulse that had begun to beat
too fast. So many things could set off this sensation of wanting to run, or wanting to stay and fight it out until the true
meaning behind everyone's words could be determined.
But this was her own mother, this woman was part of her,
and surely her mother had the right to be terribly homesick.

"And you and Paul had wanted so much to go to America.
Do you remember? You were practically babies then, and
you wanted so much to go to America because I had told
you about the hot cross buns, and shopping in Rogers Peet,
and sodas and sundaes in Schrafft's, and putting nickels in
the Automat slots, and the sightseeing tours everywhere,
and New Year's Eve in Chinatown.

"You were so eager to leave China that year—of course,
there were the air raids—that you even said (and the young

[2] EXTRATERRITORIALITY: exemption from local legal jurisdiction, such as
   is granted to foreign diplomats.

can be so hard)—that you even said it was all right to leave
daddy in Shanghai, that you simply must go to America.
Paul, you, and I must go to America, just until the 'incident,' the war, blew over. And on the *Empress of Japan*
you didn't seem to miss your daddy at all, but ate everything on that menu, and it was quite a menu.

"I don't understand you," her mother continued. "First
you wanted to go so badly, then you hated it, and now I
just don't know what you feel. I just couldn't venture a
guess at all."

She stopped suddenly in exclamation over a cart of
flowers that had spilled half its load on the sidewalk. She
must buy some from the poor vendor, and she set to picking, comparing, and bargaining. . . .

Sylvia laughed at herself, laughed at the memory of
herself as a twelve-year-old who was now, after all, only
wrapped up in eight more years of foolishness. But this
foolishness was called growing up. No wonder her poor
mother did not understand her. Who would (for Sylvia
thought of adolescence as a somewhat psychotic period
of one's life), and who wanted to achieve perfect understanding with insanity?

Her mother now laughed too, echoing Sylvia, and handed
her a bunch of roses and some young bulbs. "Aren't they
exquisite, my darling? They're American Beauty roses;
they look just like the ones I had in the garden in Nanking.
And the bulbs. You know how your father loves narcissi.
They are so delicate and Chinese. And I'll carry these,"
and the vendor filled her arms with two dozen gladioli of
assorted colors. They were still stiff with freshness, hard
flowers unfurling from the ungiving stems. They stood
away from each other, even wrapped in the funnel-shaped
paper, and as a bunch they had to be held like a brittle
package.

I'm like those gladioli, Sylvia thought, young, hard, and
ungiving still. I must learn to relax, to resist less. My
mother shouldn't threaten my existence; she doesn't mean
to; it all lies in me. And the tether seemed to give way, and

even the leavings of their conversation did not disturb her on the rest of the way home, not even when her mother said, "It was the biggest mistake of my life, returning to China in thirty-eight." And Sylvia knew she didn't mean that the mistake had anything to do with Liyi. Helen loved Liyi and would always love him. But she didn't love China (why should she?), and she did not recognize the conflict, an inheritance she did not even know that she had given her children.

But the afternoon's aura seemed to have been left at the front gate as they climbed the stairs.

"Those bulbs," Helen said, as she tossed her hat on the bed. "Give me those bulbs right away. No, no, not like that; you'll hurt them, silly. There, now, you take care of these gladioli and I'll pop these roses in here." The roses were for her bedroom, hers and Liyi's; the gladioli Sylvia arranged in two cut-glass vases (purchased one extravagant day at Jensen's) in the living room. Helen moved in quick, energetic strides up and back, left and right, the bulbs held in one hand, and soon the flowers were arranged with the greatest efficiency, while Sylvia held her breath.

Her father had been reading in the living room, waiting for his girls to return, and now rose, standing in absent-minded admiration of the surfeit of flowers. In China, flowers were not purchased only at the florist's, but even at market places, next to garlic and pigs' feet, at corners and bazaars, and they seemed to flourish in dirt and manure, in flood and drought.

"Oh." He suddenly recovered his senses. "Let me take care of the bulbs. I know just what to do with them."

"Certainly not," Helen flashed. "I'm taking care of them. I bought them, didn't I? For you. But I bought them and I'm taking care of them and you keep out of this!"

"Yes, yes, yes," and he smiled at Sylvia. "Yes, Helen, yes." Her father knew when to shunt onto a sidetrack, to bide his time. For when Helen got charged up, she was dangerous, ready to plow down anything that stood in the way of her goal.

"But," he ventured placatingly, "may I bring you a dish to put them in? Allow me to do just that much for my wife."

"Allow you nothing," Helen retorted. "I'm doing this. Stop interfering, for heaven's sake. Can't you see I'm thinking!"

There was no doubt that she was thinking, Sylvia thought, watching her eyes roam the room under the pleated brows. Until she had discharged this energy, completed the task, they would have to try not to exist, try to be invisible. If anything lay on her track before she slowed down, the accident would tear a rent in their lives.

"Out of my way," she said to Sylvia, who stood transfixed before the cabinet. "Can't you see your mother wants to get something," and she gave her a jab with her elbow. "What is the matter with you; can't you move?" She rattled the door of the cabinet, which she had locked with housewifely possessiveness just the day before.

"Get the key! Get the key!" She stamped her foot. "Do you hear me, get the key!" And Sylvia resisted an involuntary desire to jump, to run, to oblige—anything but to stand there, grinding down her nerves.

"What key?" Sylvia asked slowly, deliberately. "And where is it?"

"In the bedroom, naturally. On the bureau, with that other bunch. Hurry; my hand is getting into a cramp, holding these fool bulbs." Helen was practicing forbearance, marking time and controlling her temper with great effort.

There were seven keys entangled in paper clips and rubber bands. Sylvia told her so, raising her voice a little so it would carry into the living room. "Shall I bring them all?"

"Oh, for heaven's sake. Bring the whole bureau, but bring something quick. I can't stand here forever because of you!"

Sylvia spread the keys out on her palm and held up the palm for her mother's inspection. Helen picked one and tried to jam it into the cabinet, but it wouldn't go in. Besides, she had to use her left hand, since her right was tightly clasped about the bulbs, dripping mud and thread-like roots.

Her mouth clenched tight, she tried another and a third. "Why don't you," she cried, glaring at Sylvia, "know which key it is? You take no interest in your own home." Her vengeance reached out into the future. "You'll be sorry one day. You'll be very sorry." She turned on her heel and collided with Liyi, who held a plate in his hand. She recovered very quickly, very angrily, and said, "Give it to me quick, and don't try to be funny," snatching the dish out of his hand and clapping the bulbs onto it. Sylvia stood like a camera, receptive but incapable of moving.

Then she could see that Helen was thinking again, her eyes darting; she strode away, staring furiously at her right hand, so soiled and uncomfortable with dirt. Her whole body was contorted with rage. She strode into Paul's room —he was out riding his bicycle after the morning of rain— to put the dish on the window sill, as they always did, for Paul's room was the sunniest, his window lined with cacti and flowerpots.

Sylvia heard a strange noise, a moan perhaps, a tortured sound, and Helen stepped back into the living room. Her task had not been completed, for the dish was still in her hands. Her eyes were filmed over and fixed in anger, frustration, and confusion. Her mouth still hung open after uttering the ugly cry.

"He's sleeping in there!" she said. "Sleeping, sleeping in my house!" She flung the dish and the bulbs at Liyi. They crashed messily at his feet. "Your stupid nephew sleeping in my house. Oh, I tell you I can't stand it. I can't stand it another second." So Peiyuan, Sylvia thought, Peiyuan who now shared her brother's room, had been sleeping after his day of job-hunting. And Helen had not been able to reach the window sill beyond his bed.

"I can't stand him," she said on the point of tears, "sleeping with his big teeth showing! My house isn't my own, with him around!"

And there was Peiyuan now—not quite fully awake, standing in the doorway, understanding every word of it.

He was a rustic with an uncanny capacity for understanding anything in English that referred to him. What would her father do about this? Sylvia was afraid for him.

She was afraid, and although she knew it was a craven thing to do, she left the room and slammed her bedroom door behind her. The scene outside her window had changed. It was dusk now, but she did not notice. She was breathing in long, controlled gasps, angrily and despairingly.

Helen's explosion would resolve itself, Sylvia knew. But the thought brought her no comfort. She felt shattered, both agitated and enervated. Her mind was frozen on a single incident.

The day Peiyuan had arrived, Helen had come into the living room and stood apart. Then she had acted as though she had to invite herself to sit down. Sylvia and her brother Paul had not been able to look at her staring at Peiyuan. They knew what she saw, and knowing had made them Judases. She stared at an intruder, an unhandsome Chinese boy, disheveled from his journey, a bumpkin. Wait till she sees his bedroll, Sylvia had thought. He wasn't a city boy, and so he had worn a coarse and faded long gown, and a pair of denims under it. His feet had been dusty in canvas crepe-rubber shoes, and his cheap watch was as large as a clock on his wrist. He had the features that Helen found so antagonizing on some Chinese. Such small eyes (What's the matter with you Chinese, having such small black eyes?), the kind of Chinese nose that looked stuffed and adenoidal, and such large, uneven white teeth. The cowlick made him look unkempt, indolent, unmannered as only the Chinese could be, what with their spitting out of tramcars, picking their ears at movies, belching at meals. His whole appearance was slack, except for the activity of his eyes, bright and eager (but they were small, tight-lidded, like Korean eyes), and the mobility of his mouth (hardly ever closing upon those teeth).

Sylvia had not had to give Paul a sign to know. Their hearts had contracted slowly, and they breathed as though in secret. They could never explain their cousin Peiyuan to Helen. Even in a starched shirt and tie, he would not be transformed. He was not an idealized Chinese whom Helen might approach understanding, accepting. He was real, and their apartment had suddenly become too small.

Helen made Sylvia defensive about China. Now Sylvia remembered—in her dream last night she had been haunted by her father's eyes. They seemed to whisper as he carefully stared, carefully examined nothing at the middle distance; he was Chinese, so Chinese, she often envied him: he could afford to forget that he was. Emotions had spoken across her dream as though she were a telephone exchange; emotions turned into faces. She had been an umbrella under which they stood: Liyi and Helen. But the umbrella of herself closed in slow motion. She had then stood between Liyi and Peiyuan. She grew specific and plain. She had felt rather than seen danger among them. Morning came, and she had awakened reluctantly. . . .

Peiping, the old walled city, was her first home. Sylvia remembered a medieval incandescence flaring in all its seasons. Life there, between walls that divided and secluded and marked off in patterns of regular and irregular squares, was as fully *now* as the warm grasp of a hand, as quilts tucked thickly under the chin, as minutes spent coin by coin by an old man in the sun. She remembered childhood and hot cereal and soft-boiled eggs. She thought, tasting these again, that one's first memories should be of loving and that these should be under the Peiping sky; that one's early eyes should grow deep with looking upon that northern largeness; that one's proportions might embrace both the utter intricacy of the new moon—the thinnest shining lunar prophecy of a crescent suspended over the spring mud—and the boldness, the lustiness, the full-blown wonder of solid sunlight and blackest artesian depths— that these should be and remain and live at the young core of every adult, be the solid unwavering pivot of the unchanging child in every grown person, the point of eternal return, the memory which is the person, beyond which no history can recede!

In the northern spring, the New Year began with celebrations and red lace paper pasted on doorways and clanging of gongs, a chilly beginning in loud noises and bright colors, then warming, softening, destroying the winter stoniness of earth with March dust from the Gobi. Sandblinded, the rickshaws wore khaki hoods buttoned like upright sleeping bags, and the rain fell from heaven straight down into the foot-thick dust like closely packed nails of liquid under the hammering of thunder.

Then, the kites! Offerings to wind and sky! Octagonal or triangular, airy as a skeleton with feathery fins, or fancy as a fiery dragon with scarflike tails undulating in the wind. Fish swimming sturdily, star shapes, circles linked with tinkling wires, humble homemade rag and sticks, an unsteady clown climbing, a disembodied strip of brilliance wriggling up the sky, a shape, a form, a color—all looked into the stratosphere. . . .

In summer, the trees bloomed, acacias, lilacs, mimosas, and the bushes producing giant peonies bent over with their burdens. The house was cool, green, with shades letting in only a fragrance as distracting as a stealthy kiss. Mornings were lemon-colored, afternoons gold, the heat dry and virile, hitting one at the front door like the sound of drums. Down the streets, people hugged the shade, as though the sunlight might efface them, so deep and intensely it shone. The imperial parks and lakes were busy with families in rowboats, arrested in jungles of lotus plants; students found love in small pergolas,[3] tourists examined the white balustrades, the marble and tile, the walls encrusted with dragons, the windows cut out like peaches and pears. Cameras snapped their eyelids, making a harvest of permanent reflections, to be leafed through in other times, in other worlds. . . .

The autumn moon was the most glorious, predicting desolation, leading as it did into the dark of the year. October lingered, clear as the blue-white of a child's eye; it rested in an open movement, flowing over and above the

---

[3] PERGOLAS (pûr′gə·ləz): arbors with roofs of trelliswork on which climbing plants grow.

walls. The rancid human smell of the alleyways was washed clean, and heaven blew cool, agate colors into the leaves. The heart was released and longed for a mooring, for the sun of the year was leaving on a tide of time, and winter was wide spaces between the northern cities.

Snow on Peiping! In her thoughts, object and emotion melted into each other—the dusty plodding of camels' feet felt like the cushioning of fatigue against the long winter night. Her bedroom was a nest at the end of the long corridor of home. The Chinese seemed to have learned the art of quilt-making from the falling seams of snow blanketing a familiar nature. Hush, there was no sharpness here! Whiteness was a presence like large words written in the sky: purchase spring with minted snow! The child-in-her had thought this must be God descending in myriad white miracles. Oh, dream me, dream me, Sylvia raved as a talisman against the present. Let there be silence; the dazzling shadow of the infinite fell on those pines, those tiled roofs, that rocky earth, winter hardening, selfishly unyielding, turning its back upon the chilly human orphans and hungry dogs trotting quickly on icy feet. In wintry aspirations the spirit strengthened, under sterile moonlight were human intimacies born. So went Peiping into spring, breaking fearfully like girlhood into love, so went hamlet, village, town, city, all the explored and seminal land, peopled for so long by so many dark heads. . . .

Sylvia did not know how long she had been standing before her bedroom window. It was almost completely dark outside. The apartment was quiet, another Shanghai evening rubbing warmly against its walls.

FOR DISCUSSION

1. What characteristics of Liyi seem most "typically" Chinese?

2. What do you think are the real causes of Helen's unhappiness in Shanghai?

3. What are some of the most memorable images that arouse intense feelings in Sylvia about China?

Jeffery Paul Chan

b. 1942

Jeffery Chan was tired of doing what his elders expected him to do, as many of the younger generation of American-born Chinese still are, when he turned away from pre-medical studies to literature. "In a way I was tired of being Chinese," he said, "not because I was too conscious of the racial line—the communities of Stockton, California, where I was born, and Richmond [also in California], where I grew up, weren't that difficult for a Chinese kid. I was tired of following the crowd, because all the Chinese students I knew were pursuing such scientific, technological careers as medicine and engineering." And Jeffery's father is a dentist, a very successful one at that!

Thus in a way Jeff and his father parted company, with Jeff first changing his undergraduate concentration at the University of California at Berkeley, then finding it necessary to go far away to think things over. The year 1963–1964 found him at the University of Barcelona, tutoring pupils in English for a living while studying Spanish culture. He was happy there, but living across three cultures made him wonder more and more about who he was and why he was there.

In his own literary cultivation, Jeff would have gone on from one Anglo-American literary model to another, if his father, a Nevada railroad worker's son, had not kept reminding Jeff of their Chineseness by stubbornly refusing to talk about it. There must be something in his family's past for his father to reject so totally, and someday Jeff expects to find out more about his swashbuckling grandfather who dominated a part of the underworld in New York, and the colorful lives of his grandmother and her people in the riproaring West.

76

After his first university degree, in English and political science, he taught for a while in the Richmond school district, then in the English program at San Francisco State College, where he started work toward a graduate degree in creative writing. His interest and experience in photography also brought him in touch with the creative-arts program of the same college, and with Ramparts *magazine, then published in San Francisco.*

At present Jeff teaches in the Asian-American literature program at San Francisco State College and studies folklore at the University of California. "I want to learn more about different peoples," he has said, "and folklore helps me by opening up many doors to the different cultures." He lives in Marin County, to the north of the Golden Gate Bridge, with his wife and a daughter.

"Auntie Tsia Lays Dying"

That Peh River fishing song. That mellifluous[1] song great-auntie Tsia sang, a fishing story in three and a half rising tones, I suspect was a fraud.

Her feet had been bound when she was a child, but still she walked a straight gray path up Washington Street for a decade. After the war she retired, of course, as did so many women who were forced to earn their livelihoods in those years, standing insecure and preoccupied with their children. But then, in her late fifties, lead-gray hair and sober rayon dress, Auntie Tsia managed a tropical fish store.

Given a warm and quiet summer afternoon, when I would wrestle a chair from behind the counter, she would begin: "In the place where I was born, the old men figured the air with kites of all colors and designs shaped to please the pale winds that lived just over the hill under a pastel can-

[1] MELLIFLUOUS (mə·lĭf′lŏŏ·əs): honeyed; smooth.

77

opy of warm, warm sky. The heavens above our tiny village rang with invisibly suspended paper bells, and birds and insects and fish rose and fell against every twist of breeze. Wings were made to flap, and eyes would roll wonderfully from long paper stalks in a harness of twine. I remember, on a bright blue scrim of India it was, black and green locusts dangled in a warm moist current that rose from the empty fields, and birds rode the tails of fish whistling as the wind blew across their bamboo bones. And I as a child tried to imitate the old men, begging string, then winding rags around a stick of dried cane. I whirled my arms in furious circles, and my imitation kite flew around me like an angry bee. But the rags fell away, and I grew weary of the shrill, unchanging note. I soon left it in the fields and returned to the hillside to watch the endless pageant high above me."

Her face against the pillow, now, a clear rivulet of drool running out the corner of her mouth. In the morning the patch of wetness will wake her early, before her dreams can end, before she is completely satisfied that she has remembered everything. She sleeps so near the floor, in a ward for the dying, cold.

The story over, she would sing this fishing song, then repeat several versions about where she first heard it: on the divan of her family home—her grandfather, his father, his father's father, singing this Peh River fishing song as they trudged home, their thin legs matted with mud and silver scales, a long pole balanced at either end by two large wicker baskets weighted across their shoulders. Then, I suppose, a fish fry followed, a fish barbecue over a charcoal fire in the courtyard, the hesitant flicker of candle fire from paper lanterns strung from the roof, while all of China stood expectant and hungry just beyond the bamboo ramparts, in a phalanx[2] ten miles wide and ten deep. Or such was the unimaginable hunger she could describe before lunch.

---

[2] PHALANX (fā′lăngks): formation of persons massed close together.

The tropical fish store was located at the corner of Washington and Waverly, and caught the sun only at odd hours, over the shorter buildings across Washington Street in the mornings and Jackson Street in the afternoons. It was a dark and dusty one-room affair with dim yellow lights from the aquariums and the dull sputter of electric engines working oxygen into hundreds of glass-bound worlds on the shelves that hung from the walls. There was, too, an odor that is peculiar to Chinatown interiors, a musty sweet smell of kept and secret possessions. I think now it was Auntie Tsia herself. She rubbed a face powder into her skin concocted from baking soda, a teaspoon of witch hazel, and a wipe from the canister marked "Fu's Tiger Balm." The musk of camphor from her clothes also sweetened the room. Her face was the rough grain brown of my own hands and would become shiny and oily by closing time. Her eyes were set on the same plane as her cheekbones, and when she wore her gold-wire-framed spectacles, they seemed to protrude slightly and were black in the daylight —though when she sang, her face turned slightly to the shade, those eyes were brown, only slightly darker than her skin.

Arriving at the fish store, she carefully removed her black pillbox hat held straight by three pins, then removed her coat. There was a large maroon sweater that had once belonged to her father which she wore as a smock, rolling the sleeves up off her forearms, then pushing them past her elbows. She wasn't very tall or thick, but swaddled in her dress that reached down to the middle of her calves with thick beige stockings continuing to her slippers (which were plain with a slight heel and had the texture of felt), she was an imposing gentlewoman. Her face formed an easy triangle. Her forehead was very wide, and her eyes and cheeks supported it like vertical columns and fell away quickly to her chin, where an uneasy roll of flesh touched the high embroidered collar of her dress. The upper lip was tilted and pinched just under her small nose. She was not beautiful. But there was nothing wasted, no luxury in her entire appearance to dwell on. Her eyebrows were pale, just a line, and her hair, black with much gray, was dry and seemed brittle, pulled severely back over the crown of her head into a round bun which rested at the back of her neck. When cleaning the aquariums with Windex and ammonia, Auntie Tsia said the odor of the shop belonged to a civilization of rats that buried its dead in the mortar and brickwork of all Chinatown.

In '29, the valley has been ravaged by the fourth column of China's loyal engineers on maneuvers in the spring of their first campaign, dividing their retreat like spoils. Sweating, attenuated[3] dwarfs play at soldiering far below with tourniquets of red and yellow rags tight around both biceps, spiking the Peh River. Charges of volatile explosives, teary and unstable in the sunshine, moldy with saltpeter from the caves that serve as storage sheds, sluglike gray sticks of misshapen dynamite they plant at junctures of the river bed. Malaria and fever describe the harvest of the fall, winter, and in the spring—America.

She did have this persuasion, this passion for harmony that shaped my young curiosity with the most peculiar notions about my world at large. Everything had capacities for more; there was an explanation for every detail of our lives; everything fitted perfectly. Her reasons, though plainly definitive, were, somehow, slightly ridiculous.

We walked up Washington Street together every day of the summer, stepping past clusters of tourists, shopkeepers, shoeshine boys with their orange-crate shoeshine stands, rags hanging from their back pockets, a jabbering swarm of monkeys, and tall, white-faced trees with straw hats. Vendors, whose stalls consisted of several shelves screwed to the sides of buildings, guarded a jumble of Hong Kong miscellany, tumbling blocks, rattan finger traps, commercial pranks—rubber flowers that spit a stream of water, magnetic dogs—and sugared coconut, dry fortune cookies, almond cookies, sesame seed cookies, dried litchi nuts, and a thousand other things, pickled, glazed, roasted, or

[3] *attenuated* (ə·tĕn′yoo·āt ĭd): here, reduced in size.

embalmed, all tempting. The ingenious faces, the toppling crowds belted with cameras dangling from around their necks and shoulders; everyone parades Grant Avenue bathed in the arcade lights which turn nail polish and watchbands blue, fingers pointing, examining, the incessant chatter. "Ethel, look at these, will ya; what are they?"

Ethel is driving a bargain into the smiling moon face of a shopgirl, her indented grimace split with enthusiasm. "I want a half pound of crystal ginger, yes, crystal ginger, that's right, one half pound. Two cans of grasshoppers— won't mother just die when she sees those bugs with their hairy legs and beady black eyes?" Ethel continues breathlessly, making sure that she is understood. "And a few of those perfectly marvelous tangerines. Do you have to wash them before you eat them? (Only for good luck.) Gift wrap them, yes, gift wrap everything, please, separately, individually, in red paper."

Tirelessly, "I only sell fish," Auntie Tsia would say, inclining her head respectfully, "and food for fish, and sometimes," her two bright yellow teeth shining from beneath her drawn lips, "sometimes, homes for fish." The truth was the store never had more than two or three varieties of fish because Auntie Tsia knew very little about them and preferred to let the fish take care of themselves. There were several generations of goldfish and guppies; a platter of turtles and a pair of angelfish set prominently on the counter as a permanent display. She bought them at the Woolworth's on Stockton Street. They were very pretty, alternately striped with three black-and-pearl bands. Their private aquarium was decorated with a terra-cotta fisherman touched with bright enamels that formed his face and long, wispy beard. Brine shrimp and a few brown water snails hung in a grove of plastic sargasso where the two angelfish fed and slept. They held their flat, heart-shaped bodies vertically in the water, and when I would meet them face to face, peering through the glass, their bodies became a thin dark line, nearly invisible, while their mouths worked uneasily at swallowing their silent world whole.

The goldfish were held in several large tanks, six feet long, four feet across, and perhaps three feet deep. These unfortunate fish were overcrowded, with barely enough space to swing their ragged tails without passing a filmy appendage across the heads of their closest neighbors. I provided fresh lining for the bottom of each tank with sand from the playground. It was also my job to scoop the layer of dead fish from the surface of the water every two days with fishnets I made from coat hangers twisted into a frame with pouches made from Auntie Tsia's stockings. We joked about what to do with these blanched corpses, figuring them into a recipe for rice gruel with a crush of water snails. But, as I was always reminded, if we had ever developed a taste for them behind the dark curtain where we ate our lunch, far from the eyes of the tourists, we would never have had more than a week's supply. Then we would go hungry and have only plain rice forever.

Instead, we peddled fish to the tourists who mistakenly wandered into the shop from the Ming Bazaar around the corner, their arms full of shopping bags, bamboo footstools, a backscratcher poking out of a lady's purse; a husband, a sailor, or a man with a camera wrapped around his wrist, his red face appearing tired and cross, a bundle of embroidered slippers with red and silver threads clutched under his arms, following behind an older woman—perhaps his mother—looking hot and confused, draped in the man's heavy wool overcoat, looking for a chair to sit on.

Her companion, a large young lady with a generous bosom, in a white percale dress and a dark, wine-red sweater, a black silk skullcap tipped with a red button and folded like an envelope in her left hand, spies for a brief instant, through the aquarium, in a space framed by the dense cloud of silver guppies, the platter of green turtles with platinum backs and painted flowers.

"Turtles!" The word is foreign and fragile. "Turtles," she exclaims, the word repeated again and again, pronounced "turt-tles." She bleats, "Oouuu, I want one, I want one!" And again, "Turt-tles," asking, "Oouuu, what do they eat?"

Auntie Tsia answers from her chair behind the counter that turtles require small packages of Hartz Mountain turtle food and a teaspoon of turtle conditioner in their water, once a week.

She feeds them minced goldfish. She is fed minced gold-fish.

We have a song about the turtle in China, the Peh River turtle song, and Auntie Tsia obliges them with a short verse in three and a half rising tones that tells of the turtle as a river flower, as a green kite, while I smile happily.

And that older woman (his mother?) allows the coat to slip from her shoulders and drapes it across the counter. She takes a small package of hand cream from her purse as she examines the goldfish, kneading her swollen knuckles with this perfumed salve that smells so much like green cleaning compound in the hallways at school. She puts her hands to her face and inhales deeply. I am standing close to her as she moves to me, her hand tousling my soft black hair, curling slightly under her touch. "It's the smell of eucalyptus trees," she whispers to me, "in your hair." Smile, I smile broadly, her fingers dancing just under my nose.

What good are these old dry sticks, prescribing an herbal tea, melon soup, and ginseng root, prescribed to old women whose husbands have listlessly abandoned their marriage beds, old women who have not lost their youthful flesh about the shoulders, and reveal in their gait and delicacy that they maintain their strict regimen and evening celibacy?

"There," says Auntie Tsia, who makes her way past the open door and points down Washington Street, "on the next block, across the street. You can see. . . ."

The young lady and her husband, who is obliged to carry the turtle wrapped in several damp sheets of the *Chinese Voice*, crowd out the door behind Auntie Tsia.

"That is the Pagoda, the telephone for all of the Chinese people in Chinatown. You see the many roofs," she wheezes. "That is because the many roofs keep the building cool in summer and warm in winter."

They listen. There must be more. The man with the turtle in his hand is clearly dissatisfied, for the newspaper is rapidly disintegrating. The sweat from his hands mingles with the warm juice of the melting turtle. "But why does the roof curl up like that, at the corners?"

Auntie Tsia's face splits and divides, an ancient lacquer mask of lines, a map, and her entire expression, which seemed fenced and gated by her tiny wire-frame glasses, leaps out to them; like a child, a pure and trusting sensibility shapes her quaint accent to their ears. She lowers her voice, and her raspy explanation touches their hearts and she tells them. "When the eaves curl up, the building is happy and laughing like Ho Tai (the fat Buddha). For children, there is so much sadness when the mouth is straight or drooping. It is for them that the emperor in China many, many years ago told his builders that "everything must smile for my people, just as my people must smile for every occasion and be very happy." *Velly hoppy.* . . .

At the end of the war Auntie Tsia grew tired of her endless tenure over the fish store. She spent most of her time anticipating the return of her sons, spending even less time on the fish, which she never cared for anyway. She grew more impatient with the crowd from around the corner, the several tourists mincing up the steep hill who found the alley a plateau. Only the most daring of them would venture into the store to pester the disinterested proprietress, and even they had been misled, believing only that the fish were medicinal or somehow unusual.

"Is this a fish market? What kind of fish is that?"

"A small goldfish," she would vaguely reply.

"And that one, there, what is that?"

"That one is a large goldfish."

"Well, isn't that wonderful. Oh, but what is that big one, the yellow orange fish with the snail on its back? Just look at it!"

"It's dead."

Sweet orange squash in wax fruit became a specialty of the store after Auntie died, but that was many years later.

In a lurch of flying sheep, regressive numbers, litanies that haunt my sleep, such imagery shuts me tightly pressed against her dying. She's dying. Auntie Tsia lays dying. I feel lost, and the night becomes a tawdry marketplace of bent nails rearing up from old lumber, cellophane flags strung in a bird-nest tangle. Or I walk the daylight hours through Chinatown, down Washington Street past Portsmouth Square where we would sit with retired herbalists, Chinese waiters who do their hair with peanut oil, mothers and children, off-duty amahs[4] and their Filipino sailors. With my hands caught deep in the pockets of my coat, I think I may not be deserving. I feel very guilty. So let me try very hard to speak clearly, sparingly, so that anyone I talk to may realize that I am a little less than what my appearances suggest—but more, however, than I am willing ever to reveal. She seems aware of her moment, even now, insisting on her labored breath inside that plastic cage of wires and tubing, drawing saliva from her mouth, her nasal conduits. Bilious, acrylic, surface warm, all poisonous hues, chromium bedwork, and the attrition[5] of disease changes her flesh to sweet waxlike frosting. My ears, my ears are locked tight against her dying—a kind of familiar possession here, a weakness that escapes doing. Clearly, there is something to this Chinese dying, and the nonsense of Ho Tai, and the colors: silver, red, yellow . . . her brownness. The fish. Kites. Her dying is endless.

[4] AMAHS (ä′məz): children's nursemaids.
[5] ATTRITION (ə·trĭsh′ən): here, gradual wearing-down effect.

FOR DISCUSSION

1. What are the heroic qualities of Auntie Tsia, and what is pathetic about her?

2. Near the end of the story, the narrator says that he feels guilty. Why does he feel this way?

Shawn H. Wong

b. 1949

Shawn Wong's father was a sensitive person, fond of literature as a means of self-expression and as a means to balance his absorption in a career in technology. Shawn emerged from adolescence with a cultivated sensitivity, linguistic and otherwise, that responds fully and variedly to the world around him.

Shawn's Chinese-Americanness does not come to the surface of his poetry frequently, but he himself is aware of it. As he puts it, he writes in order to arrest a certain experience or feeling and by arresting it, intensify it, and after intensifying it, enable himself to see it and recognize it more clearly. And when he does see it clearly, he recognizes himself in it, which makes it inescapably Chinese-American because that's what he is!

"Letter to Kay Boyle" was written while Shawn was a student at San Francisco State College, during the student-faculty conflict with the administration of the school in 1968–1969. Kay Boyle, author of numerous books, short stories, and magazine articles, was then teaching at the college and was a leader in faculty support of student demands.

Shawn Wong was graduated from the University of California at Berkeley in 1971 with a bachelor's degree in English literature. He is presently teaching at San Francisco State College while working toward a master's degree.

Letter to Kay Boyle

Dear Kay, whatever generation of poets
I wish to include myself in
it must always remember their childhood
and retain a corner of the spirit.
Have you ever waded in the ocean at sunset
and thrown sand dollars over the waves?
When they hit the waves, glistening
orange winged angels
hover momentarily over their kingdom.
You forget how cold your feet are.
And the childhood spirit?
You forget that you are wearing your best pants
and your shoes are somewhere
on the beach being greeted by silent creeping waves.
Have you ever wandered
in a morning mountain mist
with flowers to guide you like stars?
The spirit must remain.
If my generation of poets are the type
that sit on their hands, stare at themselves
in mirrors and constantly remind themselves
that they are poets,
I'll be a poet in exile.
Having learned—especially from your spirit
that the hand must be a clenched firm fist
against injustice.
But you must also feel the pulsating
of the blood in the firm fist
for the heart and life line
are at the very center.

FOR DISCUSSION

What is the "spirit" in the fourth line of the poem? Is it the same
"spirit" mentioned in lines 11, 18, and 24?

Russell C. Leong

b. 1950

Russell Leong wants to travel, meet people, experience things, and write—somewhat as his father, the journalist Charles Leong, has done, and yet Russell does not quite wish to "be" his father. For one thing, Russell does not understand why his father continues to be haunted by an anxiety to capsulize his life experience into a book, an epitome of Chinese-American experience during the first half of the twentieth century.

Like many Americans of his age brought up in an urban center like San Francisco, Russell is disturbed by the multiple world and social problems and by his own unfulfilled needs, but unlike many other Chinese-Americans of his age, he has not felt any sting in his twenty years of living inside of and near San Francisco's Chinatown. He does not feel that he is a product of the neon-lighted, tourist-infested Chinese ghetto in America.

Just to learn more about what Chinatown means, Russell works as a part-time tour-conductor right there, while attending San Francisco State College, where his field of concentration is creative writing. It has been predicted that his poems, sensitively and honestly portraying his feelings now, will someday capture his unique third-generation Chinese-American experience because he is not running away from it.

Threads

There is no way to show it
No way to even break it or
Burn it or throw it away.
It is with me, and yet
There is nothing I can say
and nothing I can do that
Will make it work.

It is with me.
A fish swimming in silence
A fruit ripening on a tree
A bulging in the back of my mind
Like a fat insect caught on threads.

FOR DISCUSSION

What are some possible interpretations of the "it" in the poem?
In what way do the last four images effectively metaphorize "it"?

JAPANESE-AMERICAN LITERATURE

The lethal poison of a collective experience which set one segment of a country's population at the throat of another has had much to to with the development of Japanese-American writing. Nearly everything written by Japanese-Americans past the age of forty involves the shock of Pearl Harbor, the relocation camps which detained thousands of Japanese-Americans as "potential saboteurs" during World War II, and the lingering anti-Japanese feeling in America that even the hundreds of lives and limbs lost in Europe by the much-decorated 442nd Regiment, which consisted almost entirely of Japanese-American volunteers, could not readily neutralize.

Most of the Japanese-Americans permanently identified with their chosen land managed to survive the poison, and most of them have done so quite well. Toshio Mori's memories of those dark days, recorded in his book *Yokohama, California,* and in his other writings, are warmed perpetually by the pleasant opportunities he and his fellow Japanese-Americans enjoyed, particularly in developing a comfortable, semi-Japanese world in the East Bay community he calls his Yokohama in California. To be sure, Mori, who at times tends to sentimentalize, is not nearly as sanguine about the whole experience as is Daniel Inouye, who in proving his loyalty after Pearl Harbor, lost an arm (as one of the survivors of the 442nd Regiment) for America, and was rewarded by this "land of opportunities" with his elevation to Congress (all this is recorded with gusto in Inouye's *Journey to Washington*).

But Mori is not nearly as grim as some other Japanese-American writers; for example, John Okada, who sees in his *No-No Boy* the aftereffect of the poison taking hold of both those who went to fight the war and those who refused to go, turning both groups into something less than human because of the multiple, twisted, sense of guilt. In between these rather extreme reactions there are, of course, also straightforward tales of the relocation experience that do not overdramatize the suffering; losing one's sense of security and privacy, though admittedly bad enough, was not, after all, accompanied by physical atrocity.

Propelled by the intensity of these experiences, some Japanese-Americans have been writing, but unfortunately they have not been widely read. The anti-Japanese sentiment prevailing in the mass media during and immediately after World War II kept much of this writing from the airwaves and the press. And now that the erstwhile enemy has been democratized into an ally and a friendly feeling rides high on the advertising dollar of Japan Airlines and Toyota, it is the new crop of Japanese writers in Japan, not the generation of Yasunari Kawabata, already honored by the 1968 Nobel Prize, but the generation of Yukio Mishima, who should soon win a spot in the American literary limelight. The works of those younger Japanese writers, like Mishima, who committed hara-kiri for political reasons in November, 1970, mirror the mode and mood of life in Japan with a compelling sense of immediacy that the world at large can't afford to ignore. But the Japanese-American writer still has a relatively feeble voice.

Lawson Inada's voice, however, has risen with verve and vigor. His memories include a bit of the relocation and the bitterness of the war, but there are things more urgent and important to him than reminiscing about the rueful experience of being a "fat Jap" in a country fighting Emperor Hirohito. Being of an ethnic minority has given him certain unique experiences that add to his writing, but reading his poems gives one a feeling that Inada would be a writer no matter how his name was spelled.

In many ways the younger Japanese-American writers, born after the nightmarish 1940s, are growing up in circumstances very comparable to those of their Chinese-American counterparts. The only difference, which exerts a subtle but decisive influence, is that the Japanese-American lived through World War II feeling that other Americans associated him with a "hated monster" haunting the jungles of Leyte in the Philippines, only to find himself welcomed back into American arms as related to the most helpful ally in the Pacific and a comrade-in-arms against the tide of communism. On the other hand, the Chinese-American lived through the war trying to prove that he was not a Japanese, only to feel himself now still in need of proving that he is one kind of Chinese, à la Taiwan, not the other kind, à la Peking. The wayward ways of international politics are indeed strange. And Asian-American writers, no matter how apolitical they may try to be, cannot easily escape these forces operating on their sensibility simply because of the color of their skin.

A Brief Chronology of the Japanese in America

1869 Wakamatsu Colony formed, north of Sacramento; the first reported Japanese immigration had begun. Until 1885 the Japanese government did not allow Japanese nationals to emigrate.

1907 Gentleman's agreement established. Japan voluntarily agreed to limit emigration in return for equal treatment of school children and other Japanese in America.

1913 Alien Land Law Act passed. This act prevented aliens who were ineligible for citizenship from owning land in California.

1923 Cable Act passed. Female citizens would lose their citizenship if they married aliens not eligible for citizenship. Widowed or divorced white women could regain their citizenship, whereas widowed or divorced nisei women could not. ("Niseis" were born in the United States of immigrant Japanese parents.) This act was amended in 1931.

1924 Asian Exclusion Act, providing for the total exclusion of all "aliens ineligible for citizenship," passed.

1934   California Council on Oriental Relations, formed three years before, forced to disband because of anti-Japanese feelings.

1938   Surge of anti-Japanese feeling. This was spurred by the economics during the depression and the aggressive stance of Japan in world politics.

1941   Japanese attack on Pearl Harbor. The United States entered World War II.

1942   Presidential Executive Order issued. This order started the evacuation of all West Coast Japanese to relocation camps.

1945   Atom bombs dropped on Hiroshima and Nagasaki; end of World War II.

1946   Wartime relocation centers closed. The centers' inmates were released.

1950   McCarran Emergency Detention Act passed. It provided for detention in camps during national emergencies.

1952   McCarran-Walter Act passed. This act repealed the Asian Exclusion Act of 1924 and eliminated race as a bar to naturalization.

Toshio Mori

b. 1910

Toshio Mori revealed, in stories written in his early thirties, something other writers try for years to achieve and sometimes never do: according to William Saroyan, he has the eye of a natural-born writer, that "sees through a human being to the strange, comical, melancholy truth that changes a fool to a great solemn hero."

And under his pen there have emerged many "great solemn heroes"—the first-generation immigrants who refuse to be crushed by disillusionment in their chosen land of America, the second-generation Japanese-Americans with their unfulfilled lives and loves, the sibling rivalry among the very young and the waning hope of the very old, the whimsical wisdom of a drunkard who is soberer than any teetotaler . . . as well as the tragic fate befalling those who had to choose whether or not to fight their own friends and relatives from Japan, all because of Pearl Harbor. All of Mori's heroes hail from San Leandro, California, where he was born, and all are as truly Japanese as they are American.

In Mori's background are education in the East Bay public schools, including one where Jack London studied; self-cultivation in libraries and secondhand book stores; relocation for three years during the war; then returning to San Leandro only to find the old home no more because of the death of his mother; and the return of his veteran brother in a wheelchair. His stories have appeared in Common Ground, New Directions Annual, Writer's Forum, Matrix, Clipper, Current Life, Trek, Public Welfare, Iconograph, *and* Pacific Citizen, *and won him deserved recognition in 1943's* Best American Short Stories.

While supporting himself with a public-relations job, he is continuing his writing career and is now well into three full-length novels; one of these is Woman from Hiroshima, *soon to greet the reading world.*

In the following selection from his Yokohama, California, *we find confirmation of Saroyan's discovery about Mori's writing—young, fresh, innocent, sometimes somber, sometimes full of comedy.*

The Eggs of the World

Almost everyone in the community knew Sessue Matoi as the heavy drinker. There was seldom a time when one did not see him staggering full of drink. The trouble was that people did not know when he was sober or drunk. He was very clever when he was drunk and also very clever when sober. The people were afraid to touch him. They were afraid of this man, sober or drunk, for his tongue and brains. They dared not coax him too solicitously or make him look ridiculous as they would treat the usual tipsy gentleman. The people may have had only contempt for him, but they were afraid and silent. And Sessue Matoi did little work. We always said he practically lived on sake[1] and wit. And that was not far from truth.

I was at Mr. Hasegawa's when Sessue Matoi staggered in the house with several drinks under his belt. About the only logical reason I could think of for his visit that night was that Sessue Matoi must have known that Mr. Hasegawa carried many bottles of Japan-imported sake. There was no other business why he should pay a visit to Hasegawa's. I knew Mr. Hasegawa did not tolerate drinking bouts. He disliked riotous scenes and people.

[1] SAKE (sä′kē): liquor made from fermented rice.

95

At first I thought Mr. Hasegawa might have been afraid of this drinker, and Sessue Matoi had taken advantage of it. But this was not the case. Mr. Hasegawa was not afraid of Sessue Matoi. As I sat between the two that night, I knew I was in the fun, and as likely as any minute something would explode.

"I came to see you on a very important matter, Hasegawa," Sessue Matoi said without batting an eye. "You are in a very dangerous position. You will lose your life."

"What are you talking about?" Mr. Hasegawa said.

"You are in an egg," Sessue Matoi said. "You have seen nothing but the inside of an egg, and I feel sorry for you. I pity you."

"What are you talking about? Are you crazy?" Mr. Hasegawa said.

"I am not crazy. I see you very clearly in an egg," Sessue Matoi said. "That is very bad. Pretty soon you will be rotten."

Mr. Hasegawa was a serious fellow, not taking to laughter and gaiety. But he laughed out loud. This was ridiculous. Then he remembered Sessue Matoi was drunk.

"What about this young fellow?" Mr. Hasegawa said, pointing at me.

Sessue Matoi looked me over quizzically. He appeared to study me from all angles. Then he said, "His egg is forming. Pretty soon he must break the shell of his egg or little later will find himself too weak to do anything about it."

I said nothing. Mr. Hasegawa sat with a twinkle in his eyes.

"What about yourself, Sessue Matoi?" he said. "Do you live in an egg?"

"No," Sessue Matoi said. "An egg is when you are walled in, a prisoner within yourself. I am free; I have broken the egg long ago. You see me as I am. I am not hidden beneath a shell, and I am not enclosed in one either. I am walking on this earth with my good feet, and also I am drinking and enjoying, but am sad on seeing so many eggs in the world, unbroken, untasted, and rotten."

"Are you insulting the whole world, or are you just insulting me?" Mr. Hasegawa said.

"I am insulting no one. Look, look me in the eye, Hasegawa. See how sober I am," he said. "I am not insulting you. I love you. I love the whole world, and sober or drunk it doesn't make a bit of difference. But when I say an egg's an egg, I mean it. You can't very well break the eggs I see."

"Couldn't you break the eggs for us?" Mr. Hasegawa said. "You seem to see the eggs very well. Couldn't you go around and break the shells and make this world the hatching ground?"

"No, no!" Sessue Matoi said. "You have me wrong! I cannot break the eggs. You cannot break the eggs. You can break an egg, though."

"I don't get you," said Mr. Hasegawa.

"An egg is broken from within," said Sessue Matoi. "The shell of an egg melts by itself through heat or warmth, and it's natural and independent."

"This is ridiculous," said Mr. Hasegawa. "An egg can be broken from outside. You know very well an egg may be broken by a rap from outside."

"You can rape and assault, too," said Sessue Matoi.

"This is getting to be fantastic," Mr. Hasegawa said. "This is silly! Here we are getting all burned up over a little egg, arguing over nonsense."

"This is very important to me," Sessue Matoi said. "Probably the only thing I know about. I study egg culture twenty-four hours. I live for it."

"And for sake," Mr. Hasegawa said.

"And for sake," Sessue Matoi said.

"Shall we study about sake tonight? Shall we taste the sake and you tell me about the flavor?" Mr. Hasegawa said.

"Fine, fine, fine!" said Mr. Matoi.

Mr. Hasegawa went back in the kitchen, and we heard him moving about. Pretty soon he came back with a steaming bottle of sake. "This is Hakushika," he said.

"Fine, fine," Sessue Matoi said. "All brands are the same to me; all flavors match my flavor. When I drink, I am drinking my flavor."

Mr. Hasegawa poured him several cups, which Sessue Matoi promptly gulped down. Sessue Matoi gulped down several more. "Ah, when I drink sake, I think of the eggs in the world," he said. "All the unopened eggs in the world."

"Just what are you going to do with all these eggs lying about? Aren't you going to do something about it? Can't you put some of the eggs aside and heat them up or warm them and help break the shells from within?" Mr. Hasegawa said.

"No," Sessue Matoi said. "I am doing nothing of the sort. If I do all you think I should do, then I will have no time to sit and drink. And I must drink. I cannot go a day without drinking, because when I drink, I am really going outward, not exactly drinking, but expressing myself outwardly, talking very much and saying little, sadly and pathetically."

"Tell me, Sessue Matoi," said Mr. Hasegawa. "Are you sad at this moment? Aren't you happy in your paganistic fashion, drinking and laughing through twenty-four hours?"

"Now, you are feeling sorry for me, Hasegawa," Sessue Matoi said. "You are getting sentimental. Don't think of me in that manner. Think of me as the mess I am. I am a mess. Then laugh very hard; keep laughing very hard. Say, oh, what an egg he has opened up! Look at the shells; look at the drunk without a bottle."

"Why do you say these things?" Mr. Hasegawa said. "You are very bitter."

"I am not bitter; I am not mad at anyone," Sessue Matoi said. "But you are still talking through the eggshell."

"You are insulting me again," Mr. Hasegawa said. "Do not allow an egg to come between us."

"That is very absurd," Sessue Matoi said, rising from his chair. "You are very absurd, sir. An egg is the most important and the most disturbing thing in the world. Since you are an egg, you do not know an egg. That is sad. I say, good night, gentlemen."

Sessue Matoi in all seriousness bowed formally and then tottered to the door.

"Wait, Sessue Matoi," said Mr. Hasegawa. "You didn't tell me what you thought of the flavor of my sake."

"I did tell you," Sessue Matoi said. "I told you the flavor right along."

"That's the first time I ever heard you talking about the flavor of sake tonight," said Mr. Hasegawa.

"You misunderstand me again," said Sessue Matoi. "When you wish to taste the flavor of sake which I drank, then you must drink the flavor which I have been spouting all evening. Again, good night, gentlemen."

Again he bowed formally at the door and staggered out of the house.

I was expecting to see Mr. Hasegawa burst out laughing the minute Sessue Matoi stepped out of the house. He didn't. "I suppose he will be around in several days to taste your sake. This must happen every time he comes to see you," I said.

"No," Mr. Hasegawa said. "Strangely, this is the first time he ever walked out like that. I cannot understand him. I don't believe he will be back for a long time."

"Was he drunk or sober tonight?" I said.

"I really don't know," said Mr. Hasegawa. "He must be sober and drunk at the same time."

"Do you really think we will not see him for a while?" I said.

"Yes, I am very sure of it. To think that an egg would come between us!"

FOR DISCUSSION

1. What is the flavor of the sake, according to Sessue Matoi? How is this in accord or in conflict with his world view?

2. Is Sessue Matoi drunk or not? Why do you think so?

Daniel K. Inouye

b. 1924

There has to be such a story in the panorama of Asian-American experience; a Horatio Alger, a rags-to-riches which, however romanticized it may seem, is real and does have a place among American hearts of Asian origin.

In Journey to Washington *the firstborn son of a Japanese laborer in Hawaiian canefields reveals "the gift of discovering that there is no limit to the aspirations of an American boy," as former Vice President Hubert Humphrey said in his preface to the book. Inouye braved the racial prejudice which poisoned both the Japanese and the haoles (whites). He survived the loyalty test at Pearl Harbor and throughout the war by repeatedly volunteering for military service until he was accepted into the 442nd Regiment and left one of his arms on a European battlefield, and he finally emerged, in 1962, the first Japanese-American to be elected to the United States Senate.*

From a book festooned with glittering political bunting (prefaces by President Johnson, Vice President Humphrey, Senate Majority Leader Mansfield) we hear the eloquent voice of one who "made it," and the experiences recorded do ring true and are at times very moving.

Lawrence Elliott collaborated with Senator Inouye in the writing of the book.

One Sunday in December

The family was up by 6:30 that morning as we usually were on Sunday, to dress and have a leisurely breakfast before setting out for nine o'clock services at church. Of course anyone who has some memory of that shattering day can tell you precisely what he was doing at the moment when he suddenly realized that an era was ending, that the long and comfortable days of peace were gone, and that America and all her people had been abruptly confronted with their most deadly challenge since the founding of the Republic.

As soon as I finished brushing my teeth and pulled on my trousers, I automatically clicked on the little radio that stood on the shelf above my bed. I remember that I was buttoning my shirt and looking out the window—it would be a magnificent day; already the sun had burned off the morning haze and glowed bright in a blue sky—when the hum of the warming set gave way to a frenzied voice. "This is no test!" the voice cried out. "Pearl Harbor is being bombed by the Japanese! I repeat: this is not a test or a maneuver! Japanese war planes are attacking Oahu!"

"Papa!" I called, then froze into immobility, my fingers clutching that button. I could feel blood hammering against my temple, and behind it the unspoken protest, like a prayer—*It's not true! It* is *a test, or a mistake! It can't be true!*—but somewhere in the core of my being I knew that all my world was crumbling as I stood motionless in that little bedroom and listened to the disembodied voice of doom.

Now my father was standing in the doorway listening, caught by that special horror instantly sensed by Americans of Japanese descent as the nightmare began to unfold. There was a kind of agony on his face, and my brothers and sister, who had pushed up behind him, stopped where they were and watched him as the announcer shouted on:

". . . not a test. This is the real thing! Pearl Harbor has been hit, and now we have a report that Hickam Field and

101

Schofield Barracks have been bombed too. We can see the Japanese planes. . . ."

"Come outside!" my father said to me, and I plunged through the door after him. As my brothers John and Bob started out too, he turned and told them: "Stay with your mother!"

We stood in the warm sunshine on the south side of the house and stared out toward Pearl Harbor. Black puffs of antiaircraft smoke littered the pale sky, trailing away in a soft breeze, and we knew beyond any wild hope that this was no test, for practice rounds of antiaircraft, which we had seen a hundred times, were fleecy white. And now the dirty gray smoke of a great fire billowed up over Pearl and obscured the mountains and the horizon, and if we listened attentively, we could hear the soft *crrrump* of the bombs amid the hysterical chatter of the ack-ack.

And then we saw the planes. They came zooming up out of that sea of gray smoke, flying north toward where we stood and climbing into the bluest part of the sky, and they came in twos and threes, in neat formations, and if it hadn't been for that red ball on their wings, the rising sun of the Japanese Empire, you could easily believe that they were Americans, flying over in precise military salute.

I fell back against the building as they droned near, but my father stood rigid in the center of the sidewalk and stared up into that malignant sky, and out of the depths of his shock and torment came a tortured cry: "You fools!"

We went back into the house and the telephone was ringing. It was the secretary of the Red Cross aid station where I taught. "How soon can you be here, Dan?" he said tensely.

"I'm on my way," I told him. I felt a momentary surge of elation—he wanted me! I could do something!—and I grabbed a sweater and started for the door.

"Where are you going?" my mother cried. She was pointing vaguely out the window, toward the sky, and said, "They'll kill you."

"Let him go," my father said firmly. "He must go."

I went to embrace her. "He hasn't had breakfast," she whispered. "At least have some breakfast."

"I can't, mama. I have to go." I took a couple of pieces of bread from the table and hugged her.

"When will you be back?" she said.

"Soon. As soon as I can."

But it would be five days, a lifetime, before I came back. The kid who set out on his bicycle for the aid station at Lunalilo School that morning of December 7 was lost forever in the debris of the war's first day, lost among the dead and the dying, and when I finally did come home, I was a seventeen-year-old man.

The planes were gone as I pumped furiously toward the aid station, more than a mile away. The acrid smell of the smoke had drifted up from Pearl, and people, wide-eyed with terror, fumbling for some explanation, something to do, had spilled into the streets. What would become of them, I agonized, these thousands, suddenly rendered so vulnerable and helpless by this monstrous betrayal at the hands of their ancestral land? In those first chaotic moments, I was absolutely incapable of understanding that I was one of them, that I too had been betrayed, and all of my family.

An old Japanese grabbed the handlebars of my bike as I tried to maneuver around a cluster of people in the street. "Who did it?" he yelled at me. "Was it the Germans? It must have been the Germans!"

I shook my head, unable to speak, and tore free of him. My eyes blurred with tears, tears of pity for that old man, because he could not accept the bitter truth, tears for all these frightened people in teeming, poverty-ridden McCully and Moiliili. They had worked so hard. They had wanted so desperately to be accepted, to be good Americans. And now, in a few cataclysmic minutes, it was all undone, for in the marrow of my bones I knew that there was only deep trouble ahead. And then, pedaling along, it came to me at last that I would face that trouble too, for my eyes were shaped just like those of that poor old man in the street, and my people were only a generation removed from the land that had spawned those bombers, the land that sent them to rain destruction on America, death on Americans. And choking with emotion, I looked up into the sky and called out, "You dirty Japs!". . . .

And so I rode on, filled with grief and shame and anger, not knowing how they would receive me at the aid station, uncertain even if they would let me stay in school. All my dreams seemed to be spiraling out of reach, like the great, greasy billows of smoke from the oil fires at Pearl Harbor, and by the time I reached my destination, I carried the full and bitter burden shared by every one of the 158,000 Japanese-Americans in Hawaii: not only had our country been wantonly attacked, but our loyalty was certain to be called into question, for it took no great effort of imagination to see the hatred of many Americans for the enemy turned on us, who looked so much like him. And no matter how hard we worked to defeat him, there would always be those who would look at us and think—and some would say it aloud—"Dirty Jap."

It was past 8:30—the war was little more than half an hour old—when I reported in at the aid station, two classrooms in the Lunalilo Elementary School. I had gained the first six years of my education in this building, and before the day was out, it would be half-destroyed by our own antiaircraft shells which had failed to explode in the air. Even now confusion was in command, shouting people pushing by each other as they rushed for litters and medical supplies. Somewhere a radio voice droned on, now and then peaking with shrill excitement, and it was in one such outburst that I learned how the *Arizona* had exploded in the harbor. Many other vessels were severely hit.

And then, at 9:00 A.M., the Japanese came back. The second wave of bombers swooped around from the west, and the antiaircraft guns began thundering again. Mostly the planes hammered at military installations—Pearl, Hickam, Wheeler Field—and it was our own ack-ack that did the deadly damage in the civilian sectors. Shells, apparently fired without timed fuses, and finding no target in the sky, exploded on impact with the ground. Many came crashing into a three-by-five-block area of crowded McCully, the first only moments after the Japanese planes reappeared. It hit just three blocks from the aid station, and the explosion rattled the windows. I grabbed a litter and rounded up a couple of fellows I knew.

"Where're we going?" one yelled at me.

"Where the trouble is! Follow me!"

In a small house on the corner of Hauoli and Algaroba Streets we found our first casualties. The shell had sliced through the house. It had blown the front out, and the tokens of a lifetime—dishes, clothing, a child's bed—were strewn pathetically into the street.

I was propelled by sheerest instinct. Some small corner of my mind worried about how I'd react to what lay in that carnage—there would be no textbook cuts and bruises, and the blood would be real blood—and then I plunged in, stumbling over the debris, kicking up clouds of dust and calling, frantically calling, to anyone who might be alive in there. There was no answer. The survivors had already fled, and the one who remained would never speak again. I found her half-buried in the rubble, one of America's first civilian dead of the Second World War. One woman, all but decapitated by a piece of shrapnel, died within moments. Another, who had fallen dead at the congested corner of King and McCully, still clutched the stumps where her legs had been. And all at once it was as though I had stepped out of my skin; I moved like an automaton, hardly conscious of what I was doing and totally oblivious of myself. I felt nothing. I did what I had been taught to do, and it was only later, when those first awful hours had become part of our history, that I sickened and shuddered as the ghastly images of war flashed again and again in my mind's eye, as they do to this day. . . .

Remembering those traumatic days, the great turning point of my life, I can see how my need to become totally involved in the war effort sprang from that invidious sense of guilt, the invisible cross lashed to the back of every nisei at the instant when the first plane bearing that rising sun appeared in the sky over Pearl Harbor. In actual fact, of course, we had nothing to feel guilty about, and all rational men understood this. And still I knew of no American of Japanese descent who didn't carry this special burden, and who didn't work doubly hard because of it.

The provocations were sometimes severe. We began to hear disturbing stories of what was happening to the Japanese on the mainland. Along the West Coast, thousands of families were summarily uprooted, taken from their homes, often on twelve hours' notice, and moved to "relocation" camps on the incredible grounds that this whole class of Americans, rich and poor, alien and citizen, men, women, and children, was a security risk. Herded onto trucks and trains, they were taken inland, to places like the Santa Anita racetrack where they lived in stables within barbed-wire compounds, and in hastily erected barracks that afforded no privacy, nothing resembling a normal family life. And for what? Because they had had the bad luck to be born in Japan, or of Japanese parents.

I think that most Americans now agree that this was a dreary chapter in our history. But I believe it to be equally important that they understand that greed, as much as war hysteria, made possible this momentary triumph of the vigilante mentality. In every city and town where Japanese-Americans settled, there were those who envied their neat little farms, those who coveted their homes and gardens and jobs. And when their hour came, these human vultures struck with cunning and cruelty, offering $200 for land that was worth $2,000, $5 for a nearly new refrigerator. And stunned by this upheaval in their lives, unable to make a better arrangement in the few hours given them to settle their affairs, the nisei were forced to surrender the fruits of a lifetime's labor, for a pittance.

Had it not been for a few courageous and outspoken men, the same bitter situation might have prevailed in Hawaii. There was, as a matter of fact, some talk about evacuating all of the Japanese population from the Islands, whipped up by politicians desperate enought to capitalize on this human tragedy, and by a few unscrupulous businessmen rapacious enough to seek personal profit in it. But these ghouls were in a minority. Most Hawaiians stood by their Japanese neighbors, and some of them spoke out for them in no uncertain terms. . . .

And still we could not escape humiliation, discrimination, even internment. Immediately after Pearl Harbor, martial law was declared in the Islands, and some 1500 Japanese, mostly aliens, were rounded up and confined in special compounds. Thanks to friends, Caucasian as well as Asiatic, who vouched for their loyalty, all but 277 of these were released by the war's end. But there were bitter scars.

And even those of us whose personal liberty was never threatened felt the sting of suspicion. We felt it in the streets where white men would sneer at us as they passed. We felt it in school when we heard our friends called Jap-lovers. We felt it in our homes when military police and F.B.I. men came looking for shortwave sets, letters in code, and only the good Lord knows what else. Everywhere there were signs that admonished us to "Be American! Speak American!" . . .

FOR DISCUSSION

1. In what alternative ways could Daniel Inouye have responded to the disaster at Pearl Harbor? What do you think would have been a possible consequence of each such response?

2. What did "Be American! Speak American!" mean to the author then? What do you imagine it means to him now?

Lawson Fusao Inada

b. 1938

If "the guts of Lawson's poetry are black," as one discerning critic has observed, that may be because Inada has joined the Black and Chicano set on the west side in Fresno, California, where he was born and spent his childhood. He had no choice: it was either white on the east side or nonwhite on the west (in between runs the railroad track), and he could not stay with the Japanese, because his parents were Christian, not Buddhist. The Japanese community in pre–World War II Fresno was very much like its Hawaiian counterpart, where, as Daniel Inouye relates in Journey to Washington, the grip of old Japanese tradition was tenacious enough to make a non-Buddhist or non-Shintoist Japanese feel that he was not quite a Japanese.

His father, a dentist from a sharecropper family, and his mother, a teacher who spent her childhood in the Fresno Fish Store, together with Lawson lived in relocation camps during World War II. After the war, Inada went to Edison High School on the west side. As he puts it in his crisp voice, "The main thing then was music: Johnny Ace, The Clovers, Little Walter, etc., and on into Pres and Bird. They made me want to 'say' something.

"After a year at Fresno State I went to Cal (The Black Hawk, actually—at the corner of Turk and Hyde, San Francisco, known as the best jazz club on the West Coast in the 1950s) and saw The Lady, Bud, Miles, and Coltrane, so when I got back to State, I was studying the bass. Then Phil Levine (the poet) got me interested in writing. The bass became lost during subsequent stays in New York, New England, and the Midwest, but there are three Inadas with me now: Janet and the boys—Miles and Lowell."

The four Inadas are living in Ashland, Oregon, where Lawson teaches in the English Department of Southern Oregon College. His poems have appeared in many periodicals, including Chicago Review, New Directions Annual, Evergreen Review, Kayak, Northwest Review, *and the* San Francisco Review. *William Morrow & Co., Inc., has recently issued the first collection of Inada's poems,* Before the War. *At present he is working on another collection of poems, about which he has said, "There's a lot of ethnicity in it, a lot of yellow, a lot of black."*

FROM
West Side Songs

WHITERAMA

Catch the skyline, baby—
Security, Towne House,
P. G. & E.

Know what I mean?
That's Whiterama, baby,
the big wide screen.

SOMETHING HOLDS

Something holds
it in place.
Something keeps it
from exploding.
Otherwise, it would be
all wars rolled
into one—Mexicans
punctured on chopsticks,
Blacks gagging

on crucifixes, curses
croaking in broken
English . . .

But wait . . .

That's why the railroad
snakes through
the town like a fence.

That's why they
toss in a few
wigs and gray suits

and sit, and wait.

PURPLE

Purple
the grape.
Purple
the mind
aged
in wine.
Purple
the vine
wine
cannot
puncture.
Purple
the face
burning
on trays
of new
empty
lots of
purple
Urban Renewal.

FILIPINOS

are sharp.
That's why
they're barbers.
Sharp
trousers,
sharp
elevator shoes.
When they see
White girls
they go
"Sook sook sook sook."

CHINKS

Ching Chong Chinaman
sitting on a fence
trying to make a dollar
chop-chop all day.

"Eju-kei-shung! Eju-kei-shung!"
that's what they say.

When the War came,
they said, "We Chinese!"
When we went away,
they made sukiyaki,
saying, "Yellow all same."

When the war closed,
they stoned the Japs' homes.

Grandma would say:
"Marry a Mexican,
a Nigger, just don't
marry no Chinese."

JAPS

are great
imitators—
they stole
the Greeks'
skewers,
used them
on themselves.
Their sutras[1]
are Face
and Hide.
They hate
everyone else,
on the sly.

They play
Dr. Charley's
games—bowling,
raking,
growing forks
on lapels.
Their tongues
are yellow
with "r's,"
with "l's."

They hate
themselves,
on the sly. I
used to be
Japanese

[1] SUTRAS (sōo′trəz): scriptural texts.

FOR DISCUSSION

After rereading these poems, give a careful description of how
you think the speaker regards his own ethnic identity.

Hisaye Yamamoto

b. 1921

Her three years at Poston, the Colorado River relocation center, during World War II accentuated Hisaye Yamamoto's desire to give expression to the feelings of a Japanese-American under those trying circumstances. And she kept writing, an activity she had started when only fourteen, even publishing some of her works in the relocation-center paper, the Poston Chronicle. *Later she was further relocated to Massachusetts, hundreds of miles from her birthplace, Redondo Beach, California.*

Returning to the West Coast in 1945, she wrote for the Los Angeles Tribune, *a Black weekly, for ten years before marrying Anthony DeSoto and settling in Los Angeles, where her family has grown to seven. When asked why she wants to write, she said, "I guess I write (aside from compulsion) to reaffirm certain basic truths which seem to get lost in the shuffle from generation to generation, so that we seem destined to go on making the same mistake over and over again. If the reader is entertained, wonderful. If he learns something, that's a bonus."*

Miss Yamamoto holds a degree from Compton Junior College. Her works have appeared in Kashu Mainichi, Pacific Citizen, Rafu Shimpo, Crossroads, Sangyo Nippo, New Canadian, New Pacific, Partisan Review, Kenyon Review, Carleton Miscellany *(formerly* Furioso), Harper's Bazaar, Arizona Quarterly, *the* Catholic Worker, *and* Frontier *magazine.*

The Brown House

In California that year the strawberries were marvelous. As large as teacups, they were so juicy and sweet that Mrs. Hattori, making her annual batch of jam, found she could cut down on the sugar considerably. "I suppose this is supposed to be the compensation," she said to her husband, whom she always politely called Mr. Hattori.

"Some compensation!" Mr. Hattori answered.

At that time they were still on the best of terms. It was only later, when the season ended as it had begun, with the market price for strawberries so low nobody bothered to pick number twos, that they began quarreling for the first time in their life together. What provoked the first quarrel, and all the rest, was that Mr. Hattori, seeing no future in strawberries, began casting around for a way to make some quick cash. Word somehow came to him that there was in a neighboring town a certain house where fortunes were made overnight, and he hurried there at the first opportunity.

It happened that Mrs. Hattori and all the little Hattoris, five of them, all boys and born about a year apart, were with him when he paid his first visit to the house. When he told them to wait in the car, saying he had a little business to transact inside and would return in a trice, he truly meant what he said. He intended only to give the place a brief inspection in order to familiarize himself with it. This was at two o'clock in the afternoon, however, and when he finally made his way back to the car, the day was already so dim that he had to grope around a bit for the door handle.

The house was a large but simple clapboard, recently painted brown and relieved with white window frames, which sat under several enormous eucalyptus trees in the foreground of a few acres of asparagus. To the rear of the house was a ramshackle barn whose spacious blue roof advertised in great yellow letters a ubiquitous[1] brand of physic. Mrs. Hattori, peering toward the house with growing impatience, could not understand what was keeping her husband. She watched other cars either drive into the yard or park along the highway, and she saw all sorts of people—white, yellow, brown, and black—enter the house. Seeing very few people leave, she got the idea that her husband was attending a meeting or a party.

So she was more curious than furious that first time when Mr. Hattori got around to returning to her and the children. To her rapid questions Mr. Hattori replied slowly, pensively: it was a gambling den run by a Chinese family under cover of asparagus, he said, and he had been winning at first, but his luck had suddenly turned, and that was why he had taken so long—he had been trying to win back his original stake at least.

"How much did you lose?" Mrs. Hattori asked dully.

"Twenty-five dollars," Mr. Hattori said.

"Twenty-five dollars!" exclaimed Mrs. Hattori. "Oh, Mr. Hattori, what have you done?"

At this, as though at a prearranged signal, the baby in her arms began wailing, and the four boys in the back seat began complaining of hunger. Mr. Hattori gritted his teeth and drove on. He told himself that this being assailed on all sides by bawling, whimpering, and murderous glances was no less than he deserved. Never again, he said to himself; he had learned his lesson.

Nevertheless, his car, with his wife and children in it, was parked near the brown house again the following week. This was because he had dreamed a repulsive dream in which a fat white snake had uncoiled and slithered about, and everyone knows that a white-snake dream is a sure omen of good luck in games of chance. Even Mrs. Hattori knew this. Besides, she felt a little guilty about having nagged him so bitterly about the twenty-five dollars. So Mr. Hattori entered the brown house again on condition

[1] UBIQUITOUS (yoo·bǐk'wə·təs): being or seeming to be everywhere at the same time.

that he would return in a half hour, surely enough time to test the white snake. When he failed to return after an hour, Mrs. Hattori sent Joe, the oldest boy, to the front door to inquire after his father. A Chinese man came to open the door of the grille, looked at Joe, said, "Sorry, no kids in here," and clacked it to.

When Joe reported back to his mother, she sent him back again, and this time a Chinese woman looked out and said, "What you want, boy?" When he asked for his father, she asked him to wait, then returned with him to the car, carrying a plate of Chinese cookies. Joe, munching one thick biscuit as he led her to the car, found its flavor and texture very strange; it was unlike either its American or Japanese counterpart so that he could not decide whether he liked it or not.

Although the woman was about Mrs. Hattori's age, she immediately called the latter "mama," assuring her that Mr. Hattori would be coming soon, very soon. Mrs. Hattori, mortified, gave excessive thanks for the cookies which she would just as soon have thrown in the woman's face. Mrs. Wu, for so she introduced herself, left them after wagging her head in amazement that Mrs. Hattori, so young, should have so many children and telling her frankly, "No wonder you so skinny, mama."

"Skinny, ha!" Mrs. Hattori said to the boys. "Well, perhaps. But I'd rather be skinny than fat."

Joe, looking at the comfortable figure of Mrs. Wu going up the steps of the brown house, agreed.

Again it was dark when Mr. Hattori came back to the car, but Mrs. Hattori did not say a word. Mr. Hattori made a feeble joke about the unreliability of snakes, but his wife made no attempt to smile. About halfway home she said abruptly, "Please stop the machine, Mr. Hattori. I don't want to ride another inch with you."

"Now, mother . . ." Mr. Hattori said. "I've learned my lesson. I swear this is the last time."

"Please stop the machine, Mr. Hattori," his wife repeated.

Of course the car kept going, so Mrs. Hattori, hugging the

baby to herself with one arm, opened the door with her free hand and made as if to hop out of the moving car.

The car stopped with a lurch and Mr. Hattori, aghast, said, "Do you want to kill yourself?"

"That's a very good idea," Mrs. Hattori answered, one leg out of the door.

"Now, mother . . ." Mr. Hattori said. "I'm sorry; I was wrong to stay so long. I promise on my word of honor never to go near that house again. Come, let's go home now and get some supper."

"Supper!" said Mrs. Hattori. "Do you have any money for groceries?"

"I have enough for groceries," Mr. Hattori confessed.

Mrs. Hattori pulled her leg back in and pulled the door shut. "You see!" she cried triumphantly. "You see!"

The next time, Mrs. Wu brought out besides the cookies a paper sackful of Chinese firecrackers for the boys. "This is America," Mrs. Wu said to Mrs. Hattori. "China and Japan have war, all right, but (she shrugged) it's not our fault. You understand?"

Mrs. Hattori nodded, but she did not say anything because she did not feel her English up to the occasion.

"Never mind about the firecrackers or the war," she wanted to say. "Just inform Mr. Hattori that his family awaits without."

Suddenly Mrs. Wu, who out of the corner of her eye had been examining another car parked up the street, whispered, "Cops!" and ran back into the house as fast as she could carry her amplitude.[2] Then the windows and doors of the brown house began to spew out all kinds of people—white, yellow, brown, and black—who either got into cars and drove frantically away or ran across the street to dive into the field of tall dry weeds. Before Mrs. Hattori and the boys knew what was happening, a Negro man opened the back door of their car and jumped in to crouch at the boys' feet.

[2] AMPLITUDE (ăm′plə·to͞od): here, greatness of size.

The boys, who had never seen such a dark person at close range before, burst into terrified screams, and Mrs. Hattori began yelling too, telling the man to get out, get out. The panting man clasped his hands together and beseeched Mrs. Hattori, "Just let me hide in here until the police go away! I'm asking you to save me from jail!"

Mrs. Hattori made a quick decision. "All right," she said in her tortured English. "Go down, hide!" Then, in Japanese, she assured her sons that this man meant them no harm and ordered them to cease crying, to sit down, to behave, lest she be tempted to give them something to cry about. The policemen had been inside the house about fifteen minutes when Mr. Hattori came out. He had been thoroughly frightened, but now he managed to appear jaunty as he told his wife how he had cleverly thrust all incriminating evidence into a nearby vase of flowers and thus escaped arrest. "They searched me and told me I could go," he said. "A lot of others weren't so lucky. One lady fainted."

They were almost a mile from the brown house before the man in back said, "Thanks a million. You can let me off here."

Mr. Hattori was so surprised that the car screeched when it stopped. Mrs. Hattori hastily explained, and the man, pausing on his way out, searched for words to emphasize his gratitude. He had always been, he said, a friend of the Japanese people; he knew no race so cleanly, so well-mannered, so downright nice. As he slammed the door shut, he put his hand on the arm of Mr. Hattori, who was still dumfounded, and promised never to forget this act of kindness.

"What we got to remember," the man said, "is that we all got to die sometime. You might be a king in silk shirts or riding a white horse, but we all got to die sometime."

Mr. Hattori, starting up the car again, looked at his wife in reproach. "A *kurombo!*" he said. And again, "A *kurombo!*" He pretended to be victim to a shudder.

"You had no compunctions about that, Mr. Hattori," she reminded him, "when you were inside that house."

"That's different," Mr. Hattori said.

"How so?" Mrs. Hattori inquired.

The quarrel continued through supper at home, touching on a large variety of subjects. It ended, in the presence of the children, with Mr. Hattori beating his wife so severely that he had to take her to the doctor to have a few ribs taped. Both in their depths were dazed and shaken that things should have come to such a pass.

A few weeks after the raid, the brown house opened for business as usual, and Mr. Hattori took to going there alone. He no longer waited for weekends but found all sorts of errands to go on during the week which took him in the direction of the asparagus farm. There were nights when he did not bother to come home at all.

On one such night Mrs. Hattori confided to Joe, because he was the eldest, "Sometimes I lie awake at night and wish for death to overtake me in my sleep. That would be the easiest way." In response Joe wept, principally because he felt tears were expected of him. Mrs. Hattori, deeply moved by his evident commiseration, begged his pardon for burdening his childhood with adult sorrows. Joe was in the first grade that year, and in his sleep he dreamed mostly about school. In one dream that recurred he found himself walking in nakedness and in terrible shame among his closest schoolmates.

At last Mrs. Hattori could bear it no longer and went away. She took the baby, Sam, and the boy born before him, Ed (for the record, the other two were named Bill and Ogden), to one of her sisters living in a town about thirty miles distant. Mr. Hattori was shocked and immediately went after her, but her sister refused to let him in the house. "Monster!" this sister said to him from the other side of the door.

Defeated, Mr. Hattori returned home to reform. He worked passionately out in the fields from morning to night, he kept the house spick-and-span, he fed the remaining boys the best food he could buy, and he went out of his way to keep several miles clear of the brown house. This went on for five days, and on the sixth day, one of the Hattoris' nephews, the son of the vindictive lady with whom Mrs. Hattori was taking refuge, came to bring Mr. Hattori a message. This nephew, who was about seventeen at the time, had started smoking cigarettes when he was thirteen. He liked to wear his amorphous[3] hat on the back of his head, exposing a coiffure neatly parted in the middle which looked less like hair than like a painted wig, so unstintingly applied was the pomade which held it together. He kept his hands in his pockets, straddled the ground, and let his cigarette dangle to one side of his mouth as he said to Mr. Hattori, "Your wife's taken a powder."

The world actually turned black for an instant for Mr. Hattori as he searched giddily in his mind for another possible interpretation of this ghastly announcement. "Poison?" he queried, a tremor in his knees.

The nephew cackled with restraint. "Nope, you dope," he said. "That means she's leaving your bed and board."

"Talk in Japanese," Mr. Hattori ordered, "and quit trying to be so smart."

Abashed, the nephew took his hands out of his pockets and assisted his meager Japanese with nervous gestures. Mrs. Hattori, he managed to convey, had decided to leave Mr. Hattori permanently and had sent him to get Joe and Bill and Ogden.

"Tell her to go jump in the lake," Mr. Hattori said in English, and in Japanese, "Tell her if she wants the boys, to come back and make a home for them. That's the only way she can ever have them."

Mrs. Hattori came back with Sam and Ed that same night, not only because she had found she was unable to exist without her other sons but because the nephew had glimpsed certain things which indicated that her husband had seen the light. Life for the family became very sweet then because it had lately been so very bitter, and Mr. Hattori went nowhere near the brown house for almost a whole month. When he did resume his visits there, he

[3] AMORPHOUS (ə·môr′fəs): here, without shape or style.

spaced them frugally and remembered (although this cost him cruel effort) to stay no longer than an hour each time.

One evening Mr. Hattori came home like a madman. He sprinted up the front porch, broke into the house with a bang, and began whirling around the parlor like a human top. Mrs. Hattori dropped her mending and the boys their toys to stare at this phenomenon.

"Yippee," said Mr. Hattori, "banzai, yippee, banzai." Thereupon, he fell dizzily to the floor.

"What is it, Mr. Hattori; are you drunk?" Mrs. Hattori asked, coming to help him up.

"Better than that, mother," Mr. Hattori said, pushing her back to her chair. It was then they noticed that he was holding a brown paper bag in one hand. And from this bag, with the exaggerated ceremony of a magician pulling rabbits from a hat, he began to draw out stack after stack of green bills. These he deposited deliberately, one by one, on Mrs. Hattori's tense lap until the sack was empty and she was buried under a pile of money.

"Explain. . ." Mrs. Hattori gasped.

"I won it! In the lottery! Two thousand dollars! We're rich!" Mr. Hattori explained.

There was a hard silence in the room as everyone looked at the treasure on Mrs. Hattori's lap. Mr. Hattori gazed raptly, the boys blinked in bewilderment, and Mrs. Hattori's eyes bulged a little. Suddenly, without warning, Mrs. Hattori leaped up and vigorously brushed off the front of her clothing, letting the stacks fall where they might. For a moment she clamped her lips together fiercely and glared at her husband. But there was no wisp of steam that curled out from her nostrils and disappeared toward the ceiling; this was just a fleeting illusion that Mr. Hattori had. Then, "You have no conception, Mr. Hattori!" she hissed. "You have absolutely no conception!"

Mr. Hattori was resolute in refusing to burn the money, and Mrs. Hattori eventually adjusted herself to his keeping it. Thus, they increased their property by a new car, a new rug, and their first washing machine. Since these purchases were all made on the convenient installment plan and the two thousand dollars somehow melted away before they were aware of it, the car and the washing machine were claimed by a collection agency after a few months. The rug remained, however, as it was a fairly cheap one and had already eroded away in spots to show the bare weave beneath. By that time it had become an old habit for Mrs. Hattori and the boys to wait outside the brown house in their original car and for Joe to be commissioned periodically to go to the front door to ask for his father. Joe and his brothers did not mind the long experience too much because they had acquired a taste for Chinese cookies. Nor, really, did Mrs. Hattori, who was pregnant again. After a fashion, she became quite attached to Mrs. Wu, who, on her part, decided she had never before encountered a woman with such bleak eyes.

FOR DISCUSSION

Can you detect the author's attitude toward the Hattori family? Do you think she respects Mrs. Hattori for deciding to return to her husband and sons?

Iwao Kawakami

b. 1907

The charm of Shakespeare's and Shelley's poems spurred Iwao Kawakami to write English poetry while still a high school student in Berkeley, California, in the 1920s, and their influence is clearly discernible in some of his works, "San Bruno," for example. During his high school years his poems were published in a Japanese newspaper in San Francisco, and after graduation he was invited to join its staff. In the early 1930s Kawakami became the first editor of the Pacific Citizen, *a paper sponsored by the Japanese-American Citizens League which is now published in Los Angeles.*

He has said that after many years of journalism, his interest in poetry was rekindled by a poetry class of the University of California extension program in San Francisco in 1947, but he knew that his father's artistic and creative temperament had much to do with his own commitment to literature. The senior Kawakami, who emigrated to America in 1902, did farm work and housework and repaired bicycles for a living, but he never stopped painting, and his canvases can still be seen in some of the Japanese-American establishments.

It was during the period in the University poetry class that Kawakami developed the experimental form used in "The Room." He is presently on the English staff of the Nichi Bei Times, *a Japanese newspaper in San Francisco with which he has been associated since 1946.*

The Room

(the years have closed a door
  open it and find a room)
this, for you and your brother
  mind you now, keep it clean
A room with swinging window panes
the wind is a hand pushing against your face
you unlistening boy, standing and shivering
  wasn't influenza bad enough?
(a world shimmers before your eyes—dew on unkempt yard
  grasses, paper bubbling on rusting cans)
that useless alarm clock
  you awful, you kids—lazy, lazy
The sun is the flash of a new knife
my brother sleeps in profound dark
(dream of Minnesota—the freezing wind, the white winter)
hang up your clothes
  the mothballs drop, do not step
Here is my black cap
I hate my green velvet suit
(child, was it tragic? Child, you could not retreat with your
  back against the grammar school fence)
remember the Saturday
  the mop, the broom—dustpan, water
On this my shelf—books, magazines, folders
I know my brother's—tops, pliers, wrenches
(a truck roars over the Nevada desert—you are a dusty rider
  against a singing blue sky)
stop fighting, stop you two
  rolling all over the floor
Your bloody nose—you laugh
the helplessness of my twisted wrist
(by Lake Michigan you lit a pipe—the room is gone and
    there is
  nothing between us but a continent of smothered years)

FOR DISCUSSION

Who is the third person in the room besides the two brothers?
Do you find the juxtaposition of time and space effective?

San Bruno

Now the grass is yellow,
Now the trees are brown,
The ditch is dark and fallow
Beside the road to town.

Where is the water that bubbled
Under the gleaming rock,
And where the faces troubled
By distant sound and shock?

No bird spent from singing
And no mole blind from light—
Only the pallbearers bringing
Limp flags into night.

San Bruno is the site of the Golden Gate military cemetery.

FOR DISCUSSION

Discuss the use of the bird and the mole images in the poem.

FILIPINO-AMERICAN LITERATURE

Manilatown in San Francisco, where the Filipino immigrants congregate, is attended by conditions parallel to
those of San Francisco's Chinatown. In fact, these two
ethnic-minority communities are adjacent and even over-
lap a little. Ask Joaquin Legaspi, director of the Multi-
Service Center there, or his free-lancer friend Alfred
Robles, and they will tell you that no amount of newfangled
neon lights can cover up the dingy and seamy aspects of
the Manilatown ghetto. But the internationally recognized
short-story writer N. V. M. Gonzalez has little to say about
Manilatown because he, as a visiting celebrity in this country, lectures to a more cosmopolitan audience and is housed
in quarters with more cosmopolitan appointments.

Alfred Robles is old enough for his writings to reflect
some of the discomfort felt by a brown-skinned man in a
white-dominated society which has been fighting at different places many nonwhite groups, not only with contemp-
tuous frowns and insulting words, but also with bullets.
He did not have to live through the anti-Filipino violence
up and down the West Coast which reached its peak during
1928–1930 in order to believe the records; he has many
fresh reminders, from the Watts incident of 1965 to Vietnam.

Not all Filipino writers react against the world around
them in the same way, of course: Joaquin Legaspi, who has
spent all his adult life in this country, has grown beyond
the concern over racial discrimination which preoccupies
so many minority writers, in spite of the fact that he still
lives in Manilatown. Samuel Tagatac only very recently
started exploiting the unique qualities of his ethnic background; previously, he was content with Steinbeck and
Hemingway as models.

The characteristics of an emerging Filipino-American

literature are still very vague. First there is the problem of quantity. The volume and history of Filipino emigration to America are not as extensive as those of Chinese or Japanese emigration. While most of the immigrants of all three groups started their careers in this country with menial labor, there are relatively few Filipinos of the second or third generation who have ventured beyond the financially more rewarding lines of work, such as the technological and business fields. There is also a difference in the collective experiences of these ethnic groups in this country. The Filipinos in America have not had such a colorful background as that which produced, for example, the Fu Manchu and Charlie Chan stereotypes, if only to be disputed. There is nothing in the Filipino-American experience to compare with the Japanese relocation drama, either. It is only during the last few years that the younger Filipino-American writers have begun to look into their background and discover that their own ethnic and cultural experience should be explored.

In this exploration, even the Filipino writers back in their homeland are confronted with confusion. Authentic Filipino literature has not been adequately recorded and studied. A national Filipino consciousness, much less a style, remains to be developed. The four hundred years of Spanish rule and influence submerged native Filipino values; then came a political and cultural rebellion led by José Rizal, the national revolutionary hero and author of the only two national novels of the Philippines, which, ironically, were written in Spanish. Up to now the writers in the provinces continue to record folktales and folksongs, and they create their own writings on variations of the same themes in their own respective dialects.

The forty years of American control brought to the Philippines the English language and the beginning of a conscious effort to study literary craftsmanship. The result of this development is a generation of writers, many of them promising and brilliant, inspired by the masterpieces of Western literature to write in English, not necessarily for a Filipino audience. And lately their accomplishments have been internationally recognized. But this leaves an unanswered question: what is the *Filipino* quality of these author's works?

If there is one single issue that would provide a common ground where most of the Filipino writers, either back in the islands or here in the United States, could meet, it would be the issue of nationalism. Samuel Tagatac's attempt to capture some of the Filipinoness in himself by involving Filipino words in his writing has much to do with this sense of national identity. Joaquin Legaspi, while modestly declining any credit for his contribution to Filipino-American literature, repeatedly states his concern about the need to rejuvenate genuine Filipino culture in art and literature. And N. V. M. Gonzalez, who dismisses even the label "Filipino-American literature," nevertheless is dividing up his energy: in the morning he writes in his native tongue, Tagalog, and in the afternoon and evening he writes in English. In doing so, he too is consciously trying to explore and make use of his own national and cultural identity.

A Brief Chronology of the Filipinos in America

1907   Filipinos began coming to the United States as agricultural laborers. At this time they were subjects of the United States, and there was no restriction on their immigration. As a result, they soon became the most available supply of labor.

1915   Labor recruiting regulated. The Philippine government required that recruiting agents be licensed and labor contracts be spelled out. Repatriation was guaranteed at the employer's expense.

1920   Noticeable Filipino migration to the United States mainland. The 1920 census showed 5,603 Filipinos in San Francisco.

1924   Filipinos from Hawaii recruited to the mainland by West Coast recruiters.

1928   Attempt to exclude Filipinos from the mainland. Congressman Richard Welch of California introduced a bill with this aim. He received support from the states of Oregon and Washington, from labor unions, and from groups concerned about the ethnic composition of the United States population.

1929–1930   Rioting against Filipinos on the Pacific Coast. In October, 1929, white American workers started a riot in Exeter, in a farming area of south central California. In early 1930, violence occurred in Watsonville, California; a Filipino clubhouse was burned in Stockton. In May, 1930, in White River Valley, Washington, white farm workers fought Filipino workers because the latter worked for less pay. By the summer of 1930 anti-Filipino activities had spread to Idaho and Utah.

1930   Immigration restricted. The depression caused agitation for further restriction on all immigration. The Reed bill expressly excluded "citizens of the islands under the jurisdiction of the United States," but the admission of Filipinos to the territory of Hawaii was allowed to continue. The Philippine government expressed dissatisfaction with this practice.

1930   Census showed 56,000 Filipinos on mainland; 64,000 in Hawaii.

1931   Estimate of 60,000 Filipinos on mainland; 75,000 in Hawaii.

1932   Hawes-Cutting-Hare Bill passed. The Philippine Islands would become independent after a transition period of 15 years. During those 15 years of commonwealth status, the annual quota was set at 50 immigrants to the mainland. Separate regulations for immigration to Hawaii were established. After independence, the United States immigration laws which excluded orientals were to apply. Hawaii was always an exception; the immigration of Filipinos to Hawaii was to be regulated by the Department of the Interior according to the needs of the Islands.

1946   Philippine independence. Provisions were made for allowing the naturalization of Filipinos residing in the United States at that time.

Joaquin Legaspi

b. 1896

Joaquin Legaspi came to the United States when he was twenty-one. Before assuming the directorship of the Manilatown Multi-Service Center, a social service agency serving the Filipino community in San Francisco, he worked in the electronics field and held other jobs of various natures. But he kept writing, painting, and sculpturing, "just for self-satisfaction," all those years.

Mellowed, soft-spoken, and thoughtful, Legaspi talks like a person who has made his peace with the world but has not become complacent about its troubles. He has some strong expressions about how the younger-generation Filipinos ought to rejuvenate the native Filipino culture—literature and art—in the islands. His writings have appeared in Filipino publications in New York.

Sphinx

I like to see you as an unaffected sphinx
and I, like the sands of the desert
supporting you for the universe to see.
caravans trample over my sanctuary
as I stand guard through night and day.
and when in my fury would drive them away

130

only to drive them further into your bowels for shelter,
I burn . . . as I see them emerge in joyous banter
for I know they shall have possessed part of you,
and made you unwittingly to torment me,
but they shall tire of you and its novelty.
then—when you stand forsaken by man or beast,
I shall always be the one holding you to the immensity.

FOR DISCUSSION

Of what significance is the contrast in size between a grain of sand
and the sphinx?

Query

how silly can human intellect be,
to ask one "why don't you go back where you came from?"
can one by some sorcery return to his origin?
can we survive by remaining with a single thought and
    purpose?
can people learn caution and understanding, themselves
    with others?
can a canned foodstuff if uncanned be converted back to
    normalcy?

FOR DISCUSSION

How would you sum up the theme of the "Query"?

José García Villa

b. 1914

Have Come, Am Here, *from which the following selections are taken, appeared in 1942 and was immediately greeted by American critics with glowing praise, which rapidly spread to Europe. The famed British poet Dame Edith Sitwell said of "57," "I hold that this is one of the most wonderful short poems of our time . . . the work of a poet with a great, even an astonishing, and perfectly original gift." And when she turned to "60," she said, "This poetry springs straight from the depths of the poet's being, from his blood, from his spirit, from his experience, as a fire breaks from wood, or as a flower grows from its soil."*

Thus a new phase in Villa's literary life was launched; before that he had made himself a name, both in the Philippines and in New York, as a short-story writer, with some of his products included in the Best Short Stories *volumes edited by Edward J. O'Brien. But being a tireless and ingenious experimenter with the sinew and tone of words, Villa decided that poetry was a medium more satisfying to his talent.*

Some Filipino writers feel that Villa was completely westernized by his college education in New Mexico and New York, and they see very little of his Manila background in his recent poetry. This does not disturb Villa at all. He still fondly remembers his early life as the son of a physician who served as the chief of staff for General Aguinaldo in the Philippine revolution against Spain, but as a poet he believes that he is reponsible only to his words and their close relationship to life and life's meaning.

He has edited many magazines, won several literary prizes, and has a long list of publications, including Foot-

132

note to Youth *(1933)*, Many Voices *(1939)*, Poems *(1941)*, Volume II *(1949)*, Selected Stories *(1962)*, *and* The Essential Villa *(1965)*. *At present he lives with his wife and two children in New York, where he teaches poetry writing at the New School of Social Research.*

57

I was not young long: I met the soul early:
Who took me to God at once: and, seeing
God the Incomparable Sight, I knelt my body

Humbly: whereupon God saw the star upon
My brow: stooped to kiss it: O then the
Blinding radiance there! explosion of all

My earthness: sparks flying till I was all
Embers: long, long did God hold me: till
He arose and bade me to rise saying: Now

Go back. Now go back from where you came.
Go back: Understanding is yours now. Only
Beware: *beware!* since you and God have lovered.

FOR DISCUSSION

How would you defend the poet if he claimed that in "57" he was elevating man without downgrading God?

The way my ideas think me
Is the way I unthink God.
As in the name of heaven I make hell
That is the way the Lord says me.

And all is adventure and danger
And I roll Him off cliffs and mountains
But fast as I am to push Him off
Fast am I to reach Him below.

And it may be then His turn to push me off,
I wait breathless for that terrible second:
And if He push me not, I turn around in anger:
"O art thou the God I would have!"

Then He pushes me and I plunge down, down!
And when He comes to help me up
I put my arms around Him, saying, "Brother,
Brother." . . . This is the way we are.

FOR DISCUSSION

What do you think the speaker means by "unthink God"?

Alfred A. Robles

b. 1944

Heavy-eyebrowed and bespectacled, Alfred Robles greets you with a warm and strong handshake and ready, generous laughter in his bachelor's apartment in the old Japanese area of San Francisco. He talks freely about the Japanese motifs he has added to the interior of his modest quarters, including a piece of calligraphic art by himself, and traces their inspiration to his two years' experience in Japan, where he lived and studied with a Zen monk. "I'm very much at home with my Japanese friends here," he says, "because I grew up with them." There is something convincing in his voice—though his youthful, muscular build does not suggest a Zen monk as described in popular stories.

He enjoyed the many odd jobs he did for his Japanese friends, and for his Chinese friends as he lived, for months, in the attic of a Chinese church where he found peace and tranquility. But he has not forgotten his Filipino friends, for whom he has become more and more involved in social and educational activities in recent years. His works have appeared in Records of Art, *a literary magazine published in Japan.*

It Was a Warm Summer Day

Listen to this:

It was a warm summer day
And I was out in the park
strolling without a worry
in the world.

And I came to a bench where
a middle-aged couple sat
feeding the birds & yapping
about Vietnam & Cambodia.

They turned and looked at me
And said, "Are you Filipino?"
And I said no.

Then they asked me
if I were Mexican.
And I said no.

Then they went and asked me
if I were Japanese
And I said no.

Then they went and asked me
if I were Chinese
And I said no.
And then they started to look at
each other & the birds kept
flapping their wings
And they looked at each other
& the birds kept flapping their wings
And said, "you must be Korean."

It was a warm summer day
And I was strolling in the park
without a worry in the world
And this couple had to ask me
questions like that.

I told them to keep feeding the
birds & quit asking me any more
stupid questions like that.
And they looked at each other
again and smiled and then said, "son
we're on America's side. Come on tell
us! Where did you come from?"

I told them I clean toilets
And they got so angry at me
they called me all kinds of
names.

And they still wanted to find
out who I was and where I came
from.

They started to give me some crums
And they wanted me to open my mouth
& tell them everything.

I kept on telling them I was against
America. And they got so angry at me
& told me to go back where I came from
And I sat there lookin' at the trees
and the birds
And they just kept on yapping away
And they just kept on yapping away
louder & louder & louder, "why don't
you go back where you came from?"

I told them I jumped out of my mama's
womb & goddamn it if I could jump back
in there I do it right now.
And they got so angry at me & threw
the crums right in my face & I laughed
so hard & I laughed so hard my belly ached.
And I knew I had to be on my way 'cause I
had my belly full.

FOR DISCUSSION

1. The speaker in the poem believes he has the right to feel annoyed when he is asked to identify his ethnic heritage. What is
the basis for this right, and what are some of its necessary limitations?

2. What effect does the repetition of certain lines seem to have
on the mood of the poem?

Bayani L. Mariano

b. 1949

Bayani Mariano's first language was Tagalog, and he still speaks it with his parents at home in San Francisco's Manilatown. He came to the United States when he was seven years old and has spent most of his life so far in the Bay area. His father's tales of the hard times back in the Philippines which prompted the family to emigrate aroused Bayani's interest in writing, but he started consciously searching for the Filipino quality in himself only a few years ago, when he took part in cultural programs sponsored by local Filipino-American groups. At present he is studying at San Francisco State College. Robert Frost is Mariano's favorite poet because he believes he can "feel more intimately the music in Frost's works."

What We Know

When I have gone living and dying for some time,
Hoping for too much from what I have seen;
All goes before me as I think what I would find.

When I have seen this circumstance and that failing,
And all the past colors turn and twist—all that have been;
I am all at once like a spectator, waiting for something.

When we look to those that come after, discarding what has
gone before,
Disdaining what has become a chore;
We dare not hide those things we cannot ignore.

When we forget.
When we deny existence to what we know.
When we have stopped.
When we have taken no notice of what is really out there;
We lose a little of ourselves in things that will not go.
The best of ourselves diminish into what we do not know.

FOR DISCUSSION

What is the essence of the knowledge that is talked about in the
poem?

A Letter to Nancy

Nancy, I have watched what you have done to me.
Directing all my energies to something that could have
been.
All my desires pent up within, desires that had never seen,
Or touched.
I left you coldly shattered, knowing that you had deceived
me.

Believe me if I say that I once loved you.
Believe also that it was sincere and that it might have
grown.
There was something buried there if you had only known

Or understood.
It's gone for now, and you leave me with other things to do.

I have promised myself something at least in this life.
That I will not risk my sincerity for what I cannot be sure of.
But I know that I am capable of being able to love
At least.
I would have covered you, shading you as the night.

When I see you sometime, we will still laugh and talk.
We will still be friends, but I think that that is all.
We will still decide what has made the world fall
And rise.
But I will not know you and you will not know me as we
    walk.
I will not see you and you will not see me in the light.

FOR DISCUSSION

What does the speaker in the poem think he has learned from
Nancy? Do you think he will eventually profit from his disillusionment? Why, or why not?

N. V. M. Gonzalez

b. 1915

Nestor V. M. Gonzalez has won all the major Philippine literary awards: the Commonwealth Literary Award (1941), the Republic Award of Merit (1954), the Republic Cultural Heritage Award (1960), and the Rizal Pro Patria Award (1961). These honors do not seem lavish, though, when one considers the quantity and quality of his writing: The Winds of April *(1941),* Seven Hills Away *(1947),* Children of the Ash-covered Loam *(1954),* A Season of Grace *(1956),* The Bamboo Dancers *(1959),* Look, Stranger, on This Island Now *(1963), and others.*

The best of Gonzalez's stories present the rhythm and pulsation of the Filipinos' lives, particularly of those in the villages and frontiers freshly wrested from wild nature. The indomitable, stoic spirit of a pioneer farmer, the indestructible desire of an uneducated maidservant for her share of life and happiness, the tearless sorrow of a young mother who has just lost her infant, the feeling of loss and awe of a rustic settler suddenly plunged into an urban center . . . all are persuasively portrayed without any frills or fanfare of rhetoric.

The son of a teacher in Romblon Province, Gonzalez studied law and journalism before turning to creative writing. He has received several Rockefeller grants to travel and write on three continents. At present he is on the faculty of the University of the Philippines, and he divides his time between fiction writing and magazine editing.

142

The Morning Star

The sailor went back to the outriggered boat and returned with a lantern. It lighted up the footpath before him and his flat unshod feet. He walked in a slow, shuffling manner, the lantern in his hand swinging in rhythm.

"Can't you walk faster?" the old man shouted from the coconut grove.

Instead of saying something in reply, the sailor shuffled on, neither hastening nor slowing his gait.

"You're a turtle, that's what," said the old man.

As the sailor approached, the lantern light caught the entrance of the makeshift shelter. Then the oval of light completely engulfed the shelter, which was shaped like a pup tent and built of coconut leaves woven into loose shingles. A matting of coconut leaves was spread on the ground, and walking across it, the old man hung the lantern from a ridgepole at the far end. A woman sat in one corner, her back half-turned to the entrance.

"Now if you aren't stupid. Quite like a turtle, really," the old man said to the sailor.

"Ha?" the other said, with a twang.

The old man had expected that; there was something wrong with the sailor's tongue. "And how about the jute sacks and the blankets?" the old man said. "Didn't I tell you to get them?"

"Ha?" came the sailor's reply.

"Stop it!" said the old man, angrily. "If you weren't born that way, I'd give you a thrashing." He waved him away. "Be off! And while you are at it, bring over some water. There's no saying whether we'll find drinking water hereabouts. Would you care for supper, Marta?"

"No, thank you," said the woman in the hut.

"It'll be best to get some food ready, though," said the old man. "We've salmon in the boat."

The sailor had shuffled away, the coconut fronds on the ground rustling softly as he stepped on them.

"Bring over a tin of salmon. And also the pot of rice we have on the stove box," the old man called after the sailor.

From somewhere a bird uttered a shrill cry; and the old man spoke to the woman again. "If you'll step out of there just a while, Marta. . . ."

"I am quite comfortable here, uncle," she said.

"But you should be walking about, instead of sitting down like that."

"It seems better here," said the woman. But later she said: "All right."

"I'll build a fire," the old man said.

The bird's call came again, in a note of wild urgency. "That's the witch bird. I can tell for certain," the woman said. "They take newborn children away."

"No, it's not the witch bird," the old man said.

He gathered some dry leaves and twigs and in a minute had a fire blazing.

"Still, it's a fine time for having a baby, uncle. Isn't it?"

"It's God's will," the old man said. Marta was laughing at herself. "We'll do the best we can. Walk about, stretch your legs; hold on to a coconut trunk over there, if it hurts you so."

"I'm quite all right, uncle," said Marta.

The fire crackled, and the old man added more leaves and twigs. The blaze illumined the large boles of the coconut palms.

The clear sky peered through the fronds of the palms, but there were no stars. The night had a taut, timorous silence, disturbed only by the crackling of the fire.

The woman walked up and down, not venturing beyond the space lighted up by the fire. She was a squat, well-built woman. Her arms and legs were full-muscled, like those of a man. If she had cut her hair and worn trousers instead of a skirt, she would have passed for a man. Her distended belly and large breasts would not have made any difference.

The old man watched her with unending curiosity. Like him, she wore a field jacket, the sleeves rolled up, being too long. Her skirt was of a thick olive-drab material, made from fatigues that some American soldier had discarded.

"Is that his name printed on there?" the old man asked.

In the firelight the letters "Theodore C. Howard" could

be read in white stencils on the back of the drab green jacket.

"Oh, no, uncle," said Marta. "This isn't his. He gave me three woolen blankets, though."

"That's fair," said the old man.

"What do you mean, uncle? Please don't tease me," said Marta.

"Well, others do get more than that. For their labor, I mean. You worked as a laundry woman?"

"Yes, uncle," Marta replied. "But afterwards we lived together. Three weeks. We had a hut near Upper Mangyan. You could see the whole camp of the army from there." With her hands, she held on to her belt, a rattan string, as she spoke. "It pains so, at times. Well, I washed clothes for a living, uncle. That's what I went there for."

"Did you earn any money?"

"No, uncle. I'm never for making money. He said one day, 'Here are twenty pesos,'"[1] she said with a laugh. "He had a way of talking to me and never saying my name, as though I had no name. The others, the ones I only washed clothes for, had a nickname for me. 'Sweet Plum,' I remember. That's how they called me. 'Sweet Plum.' What's a 'plum,' uncle? They say it's a fruit."

"I don't know," said the old man. "In our country, we have no such fruit."

"He would not call me 'Sweet Plum,' even. And, as I said, he wanted to give me the money. 'What for?' I said. And he said, 'For your mother.' But I have no mother, I told him so. 'Well, for your father and brothers and sisters.' But I have no such folk. I told him so. I said, 'Keep your money. I love you, so keep your money.' And he was angry, and he swore and then left the hut. I never saw him again, but he left me three woolen blankets."

The old man listened to the story with great interest, but now that it was over, he made no comment beyond getting up and thoughtfully tending the fire.

"No, uncle. You're wrong to think I ever earned money," Marta said. She walked a few steps and returned to the

[1] PESOS (pā′sōs): coins or notes each worth about twenty-five American cents.

fireside. "By the way, uncle, how much does it cost to go to San Paulino in your boat?"

"That's where you live?"

She nodded.

"For you, nothing. Not a centavo."[2]

"I can give you one of my woolen blankets."

"The trip will cost you nothing."

"Of course, you'll say, 'What a foolish woman she is! To think that she does not know when her time comes!' But truly, uncle, the days are the same to me. The nights are the same. I can't count days and months. Maybe, uncle, I'll never grow old. Do you think I'll ever grow old?"

The old man did not know what to say. A soft chuckle, and that was all.

"And I am going home. Am I not foolish, uncle?"

To humor her, the old man said: "Yes, you are quite foolish. A good thing you found my boat, no?"

"I feel lucky, yes," Marta said. "I must leave, that was all. Maybe, it isn't my time yet. The long walk from Upper Mangyan, and then three days on the beach, before finding your boat. . . . Maybe, this is only the seventh month. How long is nine months, uncle?"

The old man wished he could give a good answer. "Nine months," he said finally.

"I understand. You old men know a lot. Now, don't laugh, uncle. I've been married before, and this man I married was an old man, too. May he rest in peace. Oh, it pains so! Here, right here!" She indicated the approximate location of the pain.

"Walking relieves it, so they say."

The leaves crackled softly on the ground as she trod upon them with her bare feet. She went back and forth, and talked on as if to amuse herself.

"Now, this man was a tailor. You see, I worked as a servant in a rich man's house. And this tailor said, one day, 'You don't have to work so hard like that, Marta. Come live with me.' Ah, you men are tricky. Aren't you, uncle?"

"Sometimes," the old man couldn't help saying. "Some

---

[2] CENTAVO (sĕn·tä′vō): coin worth one hundredth of a peso.

men are, I must say," he agreed readily.

"This tailor, he saw how industrious I was—and, I dare say, I am. Because God made me so; with the build of an animal, how can one be lazy? There's not a kind of work you men can do that I can't do also. That's a woman for you! My tailor was pleased with me. I was a woman and a man all in one, and he was so happy he stopped becoming a tailor and took instead to visiting with neighbors, talking politics and things like that." She stopped and then as if suddenly remembering something: "But he left me no child. Oh, he fooled me so, uncle!"

"Well, you'll have one soon, I must say," said the old man.

"As I was saying, I lived with this old tailor. He was a widower and had been lonely, and now he was kind to me. But he died of consumption—he had it for a long time— the year the war started. I went back to the rich man's house where I had worked before. When the Americans came back, I said to this rich man, 'I am going away. Only for a short time, though. I hear they pay well at the camp of the army, if you can wash clothes and do things like that. When I have enough money, I'll come back.' That's what I said. Oh, oh! It hurts so!"

"It's time the sailor returns," said the old man. "Does it pain much?"

"Ah, but pain never bothers me, uncle. Didn't I tell you I am built like an animal? This tailor, he used to beat me. I didn't care. I can stand anything, you know. I chopped wood and pounded rice for him. I was quite sorry when he died. That's the truth, uncle."

She stopped and laughed, amused more than ever, perhaps, at the way she had been talking. The old man looked at her quizzically.

"And you'll bring this baby home to San Paulino?" he said.

"Why, of course, uncle. It'll be so tiny, so helpless— you know. Why do you ask?"

The old man hesitated, but in the end he decided to tell her: "There are places—in the city, for example—where they'll take care of babies like that. . . ."

"But can they take care of him better than I? That's impossible, uncle," the woman said, excitedly. "Oh, it hurts so!—I do like—oh!—to look after him myself. . . ."

The firelight caught her faint smile. She had a common-looking face, but her eyes were pretty and big and smiling.

She had stopped talking. The sailor appeared in their midst, saying, "Ha!"

"Warm the salmon in the fire," said the old man.

He took the jute sacks and the blankets into the shelter and prepared a bed. Outside, in the light of the fire, the sailor opened the salmon can with his bolo[3] and began drinking the soup in the can.

"Can't you wait for me?"

The old man crawled out of the hut, annoyed partly because the sailor had begun to eat and partly because Marta was groaning.

"Don't wail there like a sow," he told her gruffly.

Then he sat before the pot of rice that the sailor brought over.

"A sow doesn't wail so, uncle," said the woman innocently.

The old man said nothing in reply. He and the sailor ate hurriedly, making noises with their mouths.

"Ha!" said the sailor, in that helpless way of his, looking in Marta's direction.

"She doesn't care for food. She said so," the old man explained. And to Marta he said: "If it's too much to bear, you may go in. We'll keep some of the salmon for you. Afterwards you'll be so hungry."

Marta followed his advice, crawling into the hut. Her head struck the lantern that hung from the ridgepole, and for a while it swung about, the oval of light dancing on the ground.

"I'll be with you in a minute," said the old man. "Why you've to let me do this, I don't know." It seemed he had become a different person from the *uncle* Marta knew a while ago; he felt the change in himself.

"Uncle," the woman called from in the shelter, "what's a man called when he does a midwife's business?"

[3] BOLO (bō'lō): long, heavy knife.

The old man was washing his mouth with water from the container the sailor had brought from their outriggered boat. When he was through, he said: "You horrible creature! I'm now sure of it! You've fooled me. You planned all this. . . . You're more clever than I thought. . . ."

There was silence in the shelter. From afar the night bird called again, clearly and hauntingly. The sailor, calling the old man's attention to the bird, said, "Ha, ha!" He pointed with his finger at the darkness, but the old man did not mind him.

The silence grew tense, although there were soft noises from the shelter, noises that the movement of feet and arms and body made upon the matting, as if a sow were indeed lying there to deliver a litter. The lantern glow fell full upon the woman's upraised knees. She had covered them with a blanket.

"Uncle!" she called frantically.

Before going in the old man looked up at the sky. There was a lone star at last, up in the heavens. He could see it through the palm fronds. He'd like to remember that. He wished he could see a moon, too, and that he knew for certain how high the tide was at the beach; for, later, he'd recall all this. But there were no other signs. There was only this star.

"I'm so frightened, uncle," Marta was saying, her voice hoarse and trembling. "And it hurts so! Uncle, it will be the death of me!"

"Stop this foolish talk," said the old man angrily. "Pray to God. He is kind," he said.

His hands and knees were shaking. He knelt beside Marta, ready to be of assistance.

"Oh—oh—oh! Uncle, I want to die, I want to die!" she cried, clutching his hand.

When the sailor heard the squall of the child, he said "Ha, ha," with joy. He wanted to see the child, but the old man told him to go away.

"Go!" the old man said, waving his arms.

The sailor returned to his sleeping place and lay as before. The night was warm and restful, and soon he was fast asleep.

The old man joined him under the coconut tree, their feet touching and pointing toward the smoldering fire. Through the palm fronds the old man could see the sky growing light, for soon it would be morning. The star peered at him as before, through the thick coconut palm leaves. It had watched over them all this time.

The old man turned, and using his arm for a pillow, tried to sleep. The sailor was snoring peacefully. The old man could see Marta in the shelter, her legs flat on the mat and the child in a bundle beside her.

The old man fell asleep thinking of the child, for it was a boy. A gust of wind woke him up, and when he opened his eyes, he did not realize at first where he was. He felt glad he had been of help to the woman, and he wondered if in any way he had been unkind to her. He wished he had not called her a sow and had been gentle with her. He sat up and saw the lantern in the shelter.

"Are you all right?" he called, for he heard the woman stir.

She did not answer but sat up, moving in a slow, deliberate way, her shadow covering the child like a blanket.

"It's the witch bird, uncle," she said in a tired, faraway voice. "Did you hear the witch bird? Now he is dead— uncle, he is dead!"

The old man lowered the lantern. It had a faint blue flame. The baby beside her was limp and gray like the blanket wrapped around it.

"You're a sow, that's what you are! God Almighty," he crossed himself, "may you have mercy on us!"

"Believe me, uncle. . . . It's the witch bird. . . ."

The sailor had wakened. He got up and sat hugging his knees and stared at the old man.

"You build a fire, turtle!" the old man shouted at him. "Don't you see it's so dark?"

"Ha!" the sailor said.

FOR DISCUSSION

What do you feel toward the young mother whose child died? Point out aspects of her character that arouse such feelings.

Samuel
Tagatac

b. 1939

His seven years in the Philippines prior to his arrival in the United States in 1946 equipped Samuel Tagatac with a good oral command of his native language and a good memory of his native place, Cavité on Manila Bay. He eventually attended high school in Santa Barbara, California, where a little blonde American girl helped him with his English pronunciation; then he spent some semesters at the University of San Francisco to prepare for a medical curriculum. Later he enrolled in the creative-writing and film program at San Francisco State College, where he is completing a lengthy documentary on the Filipinos in the Bay area. He started writing under the spell of Steinbeck and Hemingway, which shows through some of his short stories, but his more recent verses reflect a conscious effort to recapture through sound effects what is Filipino in him. He experiments with Ilo Kano words mixed with English, and he feels that he is finding more of himself in the results.

A Funeral

For Mrs. Potash

It's a bad day
For rain, I agree.
Your clean black suit
Will get soaked in spite
Of the umbrella.
A chilling wind too,
No good at all
For this chest cold
That seems to rip
My chest and lungs
At each dry taunting
Cough. But you,
It seems, have a joy
About this wetness
Wetting everything
Except the sun.

It's a bad day
For a funeral, I agree.
Or, perhaps, it is
Good in another
Sense like tears
In a lonely room
When brides for the last
Time say good-bye.

Here are my flowers.
They'll do nicely
In the grass and rain—
Better than a day
Wilting in the sun.
Here's also my arm,

A small comfort
I know, I know
I remember her too,
Turning on her aplomb
Smile as she used
To squirm in her way
Of drawing tightly
Her soft large hulk
About her rimless
Glasses, not at all
Like I pictured
Of a landlady
Stuffed with gossip
And overdue rent.

I must leave you now.
Isn't it time for you?
The long limousines
I'm sure are dry.
Don't wait for me.
Not for my sake.
For this of all things
Must be prompt and careful
As birth with a cry.

Go on! Don't wait
For me in the rain.
When it has stopped,
Your scent of mothballs
And rain will remind me
Of this time and place.

FOR DISCUSSION

Whose funeral is it? Is it important to know this in order to appreciate the poem?

J. C. Dionisio

b. 1910

J. C. Dionisio was born in Kelido, Catiz, in the Philippines, but has spent most of his adult life in America. He has traveled much and has tried a variety of jobs, but his principal career developed in the Philippine foreign service, including many years in the consulates on the U. S. West Coast. Before World War II he edited the Philippine Pioneer *in California and the* Philippine Journal, *and during that war he edited the* Bataan Correspondent. *He is now Philippine ambassador in Islamabad, West Pakistan.*

A Summer in an Alaskan Salmon Cannery

"Big Mistake" nervously paced the mess-house floor. Around him were gathered the men—towels and toothbrushes still in hand. There was tense apprehension in the air. It was 5:20 o'clock, and in ten minutes the bull cook would beat the gong. Breakfast.

We all blessed that gong when it sounded at noon and at six o'clock in the evening. But everybody cursed it at five o'clock in the morning. For its devilish sound pierced your ears no matter how deep under the covers you buried your

154

head. And when you have stood for eighteen hours in the cold, slimy fish house, you'd wish to God you were out alone on a lonely island where there were no bosses nor gongs to break your sweet dreamless sleep.

But we were not gathered there that morning to protest against the gong. It was bad enough, but we knew it was necessary. After all, they had to wake us up: we were not paid to sleep. We were gathered there because the previous day we had lodged a complaint with the boss against the Chinese cook. We let it be known that as human beings we could not stand working from six in the morning to twelve at night and be given hard rice and salted salmon for breakfast. We simply could not eat the stuff. We demanded coffee—and no salt salmon.

The cook was apparently in sympathy with us. We could understand his position well enough, but by some queer twist of human nature we blamed our lot on him. He was a Chinese and the contractor was his countryman. When Big Mistake as undelegated leader of the gang apprised him of our demand, he said absently, "I no know. You ashee boshee."

Our Filipino foreman was a middle-aged person who had been handling cannery crews for some fifteen years. He had an unusually flat nose, and his eyes closed and opened incessantly while he talked. He had a hard mouth and his face was slightly pockmarked. He seemed amiable enough, but he sided too much with the Chinese. We didn't think that was right.

Anyway, when Big Mistake approached him one morning, Louie—that was his name—anticipated him, bellowing threateningly: "I know what you want, Big Mistake. You want to complain about the chow. What do you think this is—a restaurant? a chop suey house? Why'd you come to Alaska—for vacation? Hunh!"

That night the conspiracy was hatched. We greenhorns were scared but were spurred on by the hardened old-timers. "The only way we can get our rights around this dump," Big Mistake murmured to us as we huddled in our bunks, "is to tell them where to get off. Vacation—hunh!"

If the bull cook sensed something wrong that morning, he did not show it. To be sure, he looked astonished as he saw the whole crew of a hundred twenty men seated at their tables at 5:28. "Wassa malla?" he said. "Allo come down oierly today."

Ah Shi, the cook, in badly soiled denim overalls, leaned out of the kitchen window and shouted, "Kan Kang loh!" The bull cook banged the iron bar. We grabbed our chopsticks and proceeded to eat.

Conversation was unusually dull, but the idle chatter and the noise of the chopsticks belied the tension among us. Then suddenly a voice shrilled. "Hee-ee-eep!" Simultaneously the basins containing the rice were flopped upside down on the tables, the chopsticks described arches in the air, and salt salmon and dried cabbages littered the floor.

Pandemonium reigned. A party raided the kitchen, and half of the crew was munching cupcakes, apple pies, and jelly rolls. Ah Shi ran to the cottage which served as our foreman's quarters, shouting despairingly, "Louie-ah! Louie-ah!" But Louie had already gone to the cannery.

The Chinese had barricaded themselves in their quarters. Ah Shi ran there, pounding frantically on the door. It opened a little and a hand pulled him in; but before he was entirely inside, a piece of pie, perfectly aimed, landed on his back. The volume of laughter increased. We were having a grand time.

When we came home at noon, there was a sign on the bulletin board. It read: "Anyone caught dumping food on the tables or on the floor will be shipped back to Seattle." We looked at each other, amused. We knew that was a scare. They wouldn't dare send anyone back. It was the peak of the season and they were short of men.

We noticed also an improvement in our menu. More meat was mixed with the dried cabbage. We had fried fresh salmon. Big Mistake beamed triumphantly. "Didn't I tell you?" he said. "Uh, huh!" I exulted. "So they won't give us salt salmon any more!"

Pete, our "retort boy," who had a genius for reticence, gulped down his soup. "They couldn't," he said simply, marveling at my innocence. "We threw the stuff in the creek!"

II

Joe was a gambler. He was also rumored to be a gangster. He was "a tough egg." The men were not wont to befriend him. They said they felt "clammy" when he was near. His eyes slanted just a little, giving him the appearance of a half-breed Chinese. But he had no Chinese blood in him.

It was whispered that Joe had bullet and knife wounds in his body. It was also whispered that he had killed a rival in love in his home town in the islands, and that he had come to the U. S. to escape punishment. I didn't know whether the rumors were true, but I did know he was once an inmate of San Quentin Prison in California. He told me so himself. Of the circumstances he didn't tell me.

Joe had a mercurial temperament. Easily provoked, he struck in a flash. But he was not a bully. He did not pick quarrels unless he was abused. Also, he had a redeeming sense of humor. He delighted in telling jokes—sometimes dirty, sometimes perfectly innocuous.

One afternoon—this was yet early in the season and the work was only a few hours a day—Joe was playing black-jack with the bunch. "Bulutong" Mac was the banker. (There was nothing unusual about Mac, except that despite his homely appearance, he was the only man in the bunch who had attracted the attention of Harriet, a winsome young Minnehaha). Anyway, Joe had the highest bet—twenty-five dollars. He had a couple of jacks in his hand. Mac had a seven up. Mac thought for a moment; then deftly, swiftly, he drew a card. A five. In a flash Joe's right shot out, and in its grasp gleamed a menacing eight-inch automatic knife.

Mac rolled to the floor, jumped up, and ran. Joe followed him a few paces, turned around, and darted up to his room. We were all so stunned by the suddenness of it that we stood there, our mouths agape.

Presently Joe came down, a .45 caliber gun in his hand. He was shaking with rage. But Mac was nowhere to be found. Joe ran outside. Shots rang out. We crowded in the

doorway, fearful that the worst had happened. And we saw.
There on the walk stood Joe—in his hand a smoking re-
volver, and twenty paces away lay an empty salmon can
riddled with bullets!

Late that night Big Boy and I were watching the "hook
fish" gang unloading the fish from the scows when Shorty
Aliston came running up to us, gesturing wildly. "Come
on," he panted. "Mac's fighting Indian! Mac's fighting . . .
hun . . . hun . . . Indian!"

We scrambled after him. Big Boy muttered under his
breath, "The damn fool! He should have known this is
Saturday night. He should have kept away from that crazy
girl. The boss has warned him."

"There they are!" pointed Shorty. And there they were,
but they were three. Two were Filipinos. The girl apparently had taken to her heels at the first sign of hostilities.

Joe and Mac were giving the brave a bad beating. But
he was fighting. Suddenly a right uppercut from Joe caught
the native on the jaw. He reeled, sagged, and fell to the
boardwalk. Walking over to Mac, Joe grabbed him by the
shoulders and without warning shot a similar uppercut
to his chin which knocked him completely out. "You lousy
skunk!" he swore at Mac as he dragged him home. "You'd
get into a fight over a lousy girl like that!"

And from that night on Joe and Mac were real friends.
They slept in the same hotel room in Seattle and tramped
together to California. I have not heard of them since.

III

Among the collegiate element in the crew was a handsome
young man named Licerio. For the sake of expediency we
called him, incongruously enough, Lizzy.

Lizzy belonged to an influential family in the islands. His
father held an important political post in his province. But
Lizzy, like Hardy's reddleman,[1] relinquished his better

---

[1] HARDY'S REDDLEMAN: Diggory Venn, a character in Thomas Hardy's
novel *The Return of the Native.* A reddleman provided redding (dye)
to farmers for marking their sheep.

position in life for want of an interest in it. His father wanted him to be a lawyer, but Lizzy wanted to be a "sailor on a tramp steamer." Then, discovered one day in a compromising situation with a young lady acquaintance whom he did not love, he "hotfooted it to America to escape the impending doom of inevitable marriage."

In America he developed a condescending democratic attitude towards his fellows. Fundamentally he was an aristocrat—as the term is understood in the Philippines. He was easily identified with the elevated-nose contingent. He had, however, a charm all his own. His careful speech, erect bearing, affable manners, and a certain subtle suavity suggested good breeding.

Lizzy regarded the natives (Alaskan Indians) as far below him. He didn't have anything to do with them. He worked in the warehouse with the girls. His job was to pile up the "coolers" or metal trays as soon as the girls emptied them of their salmon contents. He stood in one corner and waited for them to be emptied. He didn't even condescend to speak with the girls, and scoffed at their flirtations.

Then one day we saw him carrying some kindling for Esther. An act of chivalry, we thought. . . . But we were wrong. It was love—at least he said so. The knowing ones said it was sheer midsummer madness.

The affair continued all summer. Nobody paid any particular attention. Summer romances like that flared up, then evaporated. Nothing unusual in the canneries. Nothing unusual to the native girls who were unknowing advocates of free love. But Lizzy was getting serious. Bad. One evening while we were preparing to go back to Seattle he came up to me and said, "I think I'm going to marry Esther."

"You're what!" I was so surprised I nearly choked on the piece of apple I was eating.

"Well," he said with a naiveté that was devastating, "what's wrong with that? She's used to elemental living, and I won't have to slave to keep her. Besides, we love each other— There she is now; I'm going to speak to her." And he ran out.

That night when he came home, he dropped on his bunk,

grunting heavily. I stuck my head out of the covers and inquired, "Well, did she say yes?"

Lizzy didn't look up. "You know," he said, "there are lots of things in this world which you can't take for granted. Take Esther. When I told her I wanted to marry her, she looked at me kind of surprised and said, 'Now you're getting serious. Don't, because I won't like you if you do. . . . Let's just be like we are now. After all, we're happy while it lasts. You go your way and I'll go mine. Then we'll remember each other—live in sweet memories.' That's all. And she kissed me and ran away. And after all we've done—"

"Never mind that," I interrupted. "You'll forget her when you get back down below."

"Forget her? Believe me or don't, you'll never see me in Alaska again."

And I never did.

FOR DISCUSSION

In each of the three episodes of this account, the narrator describes a conflict that took place. Which conflict do you think teaches the most valuable lesson, and why?

Bienvenido N. Santos

b. 1911

---

*Bienvenido Santos spent his World War II years in the
United States, acquiring advanced education first at the
University of Illinois, then at Columbia and Harvard, and
then traveling under United States Government sponsor-
ship to give talks on Philippine culture and meet Filipinos
in this country. Those years saw a great change in him:
a popular storyteller describing charming, unaffected,
simple folk in his tales before he left the islands, he returned to his homeland sad and disheartened, more
matured as a writer, to be sure, but full of stories about
his lonely and lost fellow exiles in America. He continued
to write. Among his publications are a collection of his
stories,* You Lovely People *(1956), and a volume of verse,*
The Wounded Stag and Other Poems *(1956).*

*Santos's early education was through the public schools
and the University of the Philippines in his home town,
Manila. For years he served as president of the Legaspi
Colleges before accepting a Rockefeller and a Guggenheim
award in 1957 to devote himself full time to fiction writing.
In 1965 he was honored with the Philippine Republic
Cultural Heritage Award.*

Scent of Apples

When I arrived in Kalamazoo, it was October and the war was still on. Gold and silver stars hung on pennants above silent windows of white and brick-red cottages. In a back yard an old man burned leaves and twigs while a gray-haired woman sat on the porch, her red hands quiet on her lap, watching the smoke rising above the elms, both of them thinking the same thought, perhaps, about a tall, grinning boy with blue eyes and flying hair who went out to war; where could he be now this month when leaves were turning into gold and the fragrance of gathered apples was in the wind?

It was a cold night when I left my room at the hotel for a usual speaking engagement. I walked but a little way. A heavy wind coming up from Lake Michigan was icy on the face. It felt like winter straying early in the northern woodlands. Under the lampposts the leaves shone like bronze. And they rolled the pavements like the ghost feet of a thousand autumns long dead, long before the boys left for faraway lands without great icy winds and promise of winter early in the air, lands without apple trees, *the singing and the gold!*

It was the same night I met Celestino Fabia, "just a Filipino farmer," as he called himself, who had a farm about thirty miles east of Kalamazoo.

"You came all that way on a night like this just to hear me talk?" I asked.

"I've seen no Filipino for so many years now," he answered quickly. "So when I saw your name in the papers where it says you come from the islands and that you're going to talk, I come right away."

Earlier that night I had addressed a college crowd, mostly women. It appeared that they wanted me to talk about my country; they wanted me to tell them things about it because my country had become a lost country. Everywhere

162

in the land the enemy stalked. Over it a great silence hung; and their boys were there, unheard from, or they were on their way to some little-known island in the Pacific, young boys all, hardly men, thinking of harvest moons and smell of forest fire.

It was not hard talking about our own people. I knew them well and I loved them. And they seemed so far away during those terrible years that I must have spoken of them with a little fervor, a little nostalgia.

In the open forum that followed, the audience wanted to know whether there was much difference between our women and the American women. I tried to answer the question as best as I could, saying, among other things, that I did not know much about American women except that they looked friendly, but differences or similarities in inner qualities such as naturally belonged to the heart or to the mind, I could only speak about with vagueness.

While I was trying to explain away the fact that it was not easy to make comparisons, a man rose from the rear of the hall, wanting to say something. In the distance, he looked slight and old and very brown. Even before he spoke, I knew that he was, like me, a Filipino.

"I'm a Filipino," he began, loud and clear, in a voice that seemed used to wide open spaces. "I'm just a Filipino farmer out in the country." He waved his hand towards the door. "I left the Philippines more than twenty years ago and have never been back. Never will, perhaps. I want to find out, sir, are our Filipino women the same like they were twenty years ago?"

As he sat down, the hall filled with voices, hushed and intrigued. I weighed my answer carefully. I did not want to tell a lie, yet I did not want to say anything that would seem platitudinous, insincere. But more important than these considerations, it seemed to me that moment as I looked towards my countryman, I must give him an answer that would not make him so unhappy. Surely, all these years, he must have held on to certain ideals, certain beliefs, even illusions peculiar to the exile.

"First," I said as the voices gradually died down and every eye seemed upon me. "First, tell me what our women were like twenty years ago."

The man stood to answer. "Yes," he said, "you're too young. . . . Twenty years ago our women were nice, they were modest, they wore their hair long, they dressed proper and went for no monkey business. They were natural, they went to church regular, and they were faithful." He had spoken slowly, and now, in what seemed like an afterthought, added, "It's the men who ain't."

Now I knew what I was going to say.

"Well," I began, "it will interest you to know that our women have changed—but definitely! The change, however, has been on the outside only. Inside, here," pointing to the heart, "they are the same as they were twenty years ago, God-fearing, faithful, modest, and *nice.*"

The man was visibly moved. "I'm very happy, sir," he said, in the manner of one who, having stakes on the land, had found no cause to regret one's sentimental investment.

After this, everything that was said and done in that hall that night seemed like an anticlimax; and later, as we walked outside, he gave me his name and told me of his farm thirty miles east of the city.

We had stopped at the main entrance of the hotel lobby. We had not talked very much on the way. As a matter of fact, we were never alone. Kindly American friends talked to us, asked us questions, said good night. So now I asked him whether he cared to step into the lobby with me and talk shop.

"No, thank you," he said, "you are tired. And I don't want to stay out too late."

"Yes, you live very far."

"I got a car," he said; "besides. . . ."

Now he smiled, he truly smiled. All night I had been watching his face, and I wondered when he was going to smile.

"Will you do me a favor, please," he continued, smiling almost sweetly. "I want you to have dinner with my family out in the country. I'd call for you tomorrow afternoon, then drive you back. Will that be all right?"

"Of course," I said. "I'd love to meet your family." I was leaving Kalamazoo for Muncie, Indiana, in two days. There was plenty of time.

"You will make my wife very happy," he said.

"You flatter me."

"Honest. She'll be very happy. Ruth is a country girl and hasn't met many Filipinos. I mean Filipinos younger than I, cleaner-looking. We're just poor farmer folks, you know, and we don't get to town very often. Roger, that's my boy, he goes to school in town. A bus takes him early in the morning and he's back in the afternoon. He's a nice boy."

"I bet he is. I've seen the children of some of the boys by their American wives, and the boys are tall, taller than the father, and very good looking."

"Roger, he'd be tall. You'll like him."

Then he said good-bye, and I waved to him as he disappeared in the darkness.

The next day he came, at about three in the afternoon. There was a mild, ineffectual sun shining; and it was not too cold. He was wearing an old brown tweed jacket and worsted trousers to match. His shoes were polished, and although the green of his tie seemed faded, a colored shirt hardly accentuated it. He looked younger than he appeared the night before, now that he was clean-shaven and seemed ready to go to a party. He was grinning as we met.

"Oh, Ruth can't believe it. She can't believe it," he kept repeating as he led me to his car—a nondescript thing in faded black that had known better days and many hands. "I says to her, I'm bringing you a first-class Filipino, and she says, aw, go away, quit kidding, there's no such thing as first-class Filipino. But Roger, that's my boy, he believed me immediately. What's he like, daddy, he asks. Oh, you will see, I says, he's first-class. Like you, daddy? No, no, I laugh at him, your daddy ain't first-class. Aw, but you are, daddy, he says. So you can see what a nice boy he is, so innocent. Then Ruth starts griping about the house, but the house is a mess, she says. True it's a mess, it's always a mess, but you don't mind, do you? We're poor folks, you know."

The trip seemed interminable. We passed through narrow lanes and disappeared into thickets, and came out on barren land overgrown with weeds in places. All around were dead leaves and dry earth. In the distance were apple trees.

"Aren't those apple trees?" I asked, wanting to be sure.

"Yes, those are apple trees," he replied. "Do you like apples? I got lots of 'em. I got an apple orchard. I'll show you."

All the beauty of the afternoon seemed in the distance, on the hills, in the dull soft sky.

"Those trees are beautiful on the hills," I said.

"Autumn's a lovely season. The trees are getting ready to die, and they show their color, proud-like."

"No such thing in our own country," I said.

That remark seemed unkind, I realized later. It touched him off on a long deserted tangent, but ever there, perhaps. How many times did the lonely mind take unpleasant detours away from the familiar winding lanes towards home for fear of this, the remembered hurt, the long-lost youth, the grim shadows of the years; how many times indeed, only the exile knows.

It was a rugged road we were traveling, and the car made so much noise that I could not hear everything he said, but I understood him. He was telling his story for the first time in many years. He was remembering his own youth. He was thinking of home. In these odd moments there seemed no cause for fear, no cause at all, no pain. That would come later. In the night perhaps. Or lonely on the farm under the apple trees.

In this old Visayan town, the streets are narrow and dirty and strewn with coral shells. You have been there? You could not have missed our house; it was the biggest in town, one of the oldest; ours was a big family. The house stood right on the edge of the street. A door opened heavily and you enter a dark hall leading to the stairs. There is the

*smell of chickens roosting on the low-topped walls; there
is the familiar sound they make, and you grope your way up
a massive staircase, the banisters smooth upon the trembling hand. Such nights, they are no better than the days;
windows are closed against the sun; they close heavily.*

*Mother sits in her corner looking very white and sick.
This was her world, her domain. In all these years I cannot
remember the sound of her voice. Father was different. He
moved about. He shouted. He ranted. He lived in the past
and talked of honor as though it were the only thing.*

*I was born in that house. I grew up there into a pampered
brat. I was mean. One day I broke their hearts. I saw
mother cry wordlessly as father heaped his curses upon me
and drove me out of the house, the gate closing heavily
after. me. And my brothers and sisters took up my father's
hate for me and multiplied it numberless times in their
own broken hearts. I was no good.*

*But sometimes, you know, I miss that house, the roosting
chickens on the low-topped walls. I miss my brothers and
sisters. Mother sitting in her chair, looking like a pale
ghost in a corner of the room. I would remember the great
live posts, massive tree trunks from the forests. Leafy
plants grow on the sides, buds pointing downwards,
wilted and died before they could become flowers. As they
fell on the floor, father bent to pick them and throw them
out into the coral streets. His hands were strong; I have
kissed those hands . . . many times, many times. . . .*

Finally, we rounded a deep curve and suddenly came
upon a shanty, all but ready to crumble in a heap on the
ground; its plastered walls were rotting away, the floor was
hardly a foot from the ground. I thought of the cottages of
the poor colored folk in the South, the hovels of the poor
everywhere in the land. This one stood all by itself as
though by common consent all the folk that used to live
here had decided to stay away, despising it, ashamed of it.
Even the lovely season could not color it with beauty.

A dog barked loudly as we approached. A fat blonde
woman stood at the door with a little boy by her side.
Roger seemed newly scrubbed. He hardly took his eyes

off me. Ruth had a clean apron around her shapeless waist. Now, as she shook my hands in sincere delight, I noticed shamefacedly (that I should notice) how rough her hands, how coarse and red with labor, how ugly! She was no longer young and her smile was pathetic.

As we stepped inside and the door closed behind us, immediately I was aware of the familiar scent of apples. The room was bare except for a few ancient pieces of secondhand furniture. In the middle of the room stood a stove to keep the family warm in winter. The walls were bare. Over the dining table hung a lamp yet unlighted.

Ruth got busy with the drinks. She kept coming in and out of a rear room that must have been the kitchen, and soon the table was heavy with food, fried chicken legs and rice, and green peas and corn on the ear. Even as we ate, Ruth kept standing and going to the kitchen for more food. Roger ate like a little gentleman.

"Isn't he nice looking?" his father asked.

"You are a handsome boy, Roger," I said.

The boy smiled at me. "You look like daddy," he said.

Afterwards I noticed an old picture leaning on the top of a dresser and stood to pick it up. It was yellow and soiled with many fingerings. The faded figure of a woman in Philippine dress could yet be distinguished, although the face had become a blur.

"Your . . ." I began.

"I don't know who she is," Fabia hastened to say. "I picked that picture many years ago in a room on La Salle Street in Chicago. I have often wondered who she is."

"The face wasn't a blur in the beginning?"

"Oh, no. It was a young face and good."

Ruth came with a plate full of apples.

"Ah," I cried, picking out a ripe one, "I've been thinking where all the scent of apples came from. The room is full of it."

"I'll show you," said Fabia.

He showed me a back room, not very big. It was half full of apples.

"Every day," he explained, "I take some of them to town

to sell to the groceries. Prices have been low. I've been losing on the trips."

"These apples will spoil," I said.

"We'll feed them to the pigs."

Then he showed me around the farm. It was twilight now, and the apple trees stood bare against a glowing western sky. In apple-blossom time it must be lovely here, I thought. But what about winter time?

One day, according to Fabia, a few years ago, before Roger was born, he had an attack of acute appendicitis. It was deep winter. The snow lay heavy everywhere. Ruth was pregnant and none too well herself. At first she did not know what to do. She bundled him in warm clothing and put him on a cot near the stove. She shoveled the snow from their front door and practically carried the suffering man on her shoulders, dragging him through the newly made path towards the road, where they waited for the U.S. Mail car to pass. Meanwhile snowflakes poured all over them, and she kept rubbing the man's arms and legs as she herself nearly froze to death.

"Go back to the house, Ruth!" her husband cried, "you'll freeze to death."

But she clung to him wordlessly. Even as she massaged his arms and legs, her tears rolled down her cheeks. "I won't leave you, I won't leave you," she repeated.

Finally the U.S. Mail car arrived. The mailman, who knew them well, helped them board the car, and without stopping on his usual route, took the sick man and his wife direct to the nearest hospital.

Ruth stayed in the hospital with Fabia. She slept in a corridor outside the patients' ward and in the daytime helped in scrubbing the floor and washing the dishes and cleaning the men's things. They didn't have enough money, and Ruth was willing to work like a slave.

"Ruth's a nice girl," said Fabia. "Like our own Filipino women."

Before nightfall, he took me back to the hotel. Ruth and Roger stood at the door holding hands and smiling at me.

From inside the room of the shanty, a low light flickered. I had a last glimpse of the apple trees in the orchard under the darkened sky as Fabia backed up the car. And soon we were on our way back to town. The dog had started barking. We could hear it for some time, until finally we could not hear it any more, and all was darkness around us, except where the headlamps revealed a stretch of road leading somewhere.

Fabia did not talk this time. I didn't seem to have anything to say myself. But when finally we came to the hotel and I got down, Fabia said, "Well, I guess I won't be seeing you again."

It was dimly lighted in front of the hotel and I could hardly see Fabia's face. Without getting off the car, he moved to where I had sat, and I saw him extend his hand. I gripped it.

"Tell Ruth and Roger," I said, "I love them."

He dropped my hand quickly. "They'll be waiting for me now," he said.

"Look," I said, not knowing why I said it, "one of these days, very soon, I hope, I'll be going home. I could go to your town."

"No," he said softly, sounding very much defeated but brave. "Thanks a lot. But you see, nobody would remember me now."

Then he started the car, and as it moved away, he waved his hand.

"Good-bye," I said, waving back into the darkness. And suddenly the night was cold like winter straying early in these northern woodlands.

I hurried inside. There was a train the next morning that left for Muncie, Indiana, at a quarter after eight.

FOR DISCUSSION

1. What was subtly communicated between the two "exiles," one an intellectual, the other a farmer, with regard to their common

and different feelings about their homeland?

2. Why was the discussion of an idealized image of Philippine women the highlight of the narrator's experiences those two days, and how was its importance enforced by the appearance of Ruth, a blonde American woman?

Oscar F. Peñaranda

b. 1944

Behind the tall, handsome, and youthful appearance of Oscar Peñaranda there hides the sense of urgency that propels him to write, and to this sense of urgency he himself is the "Lone Witness"—a poem he wrote in August, 1970:

> "... I must!
> I am old
> I'm fast clearing twenty-five years and
> I've got a lot of things to say
> that's never before been said."

"The Price" is not the only kind of story he wishes to tell, but he wants to tell enough of this type before focusing his attention on something else. He has a sense of obligation to, and more importantly, a deep perception of, the life of his people in Leyte Province of the Philippines, where he spent his first thirteen years before moving to Canada with his parents. In writing he is consciously striving to integrate his Filipino sensitivity with his life in America, which is far removed from that of the islands. At the present time Mr. Peñaranda is living in San Francisco, where he has a teaching assignment in the Filipino-American literature program of San Francisco State College. Since his arrival in the San Francisco area, he has been passing the summers with odd jobs up and down the West Coast, from Alaskan canneries to San Joaquin Valley farms.

172

The Price

Every time my fragile Uncle Andres came to the house, someone would almost always end up arguing with him about the ideas he had concerning his land. This someone would almost always be my father. And because it was my father's house, Uncle Andres would always leave before the argument got too hot and the name-calling started. He would exit respectfully with a bow, smoothing his curled-up moustache. Everyone knew my uncle's stand was hopeless. He himself must have had glimpses of it.

First of all, the land was too close to the city Tacloban, where only cement grew. Secondly, the Community Board was bent on building a road through the land, for our town, Santander, was blossoming into urbanic stature and it, our town, was feeling its muscles.

They didn't look like brothers at all, my uncle and my father. My father was stout, clean-shaven, well-dressed, and streaks of gray hair spread abundantly over his light-brown round face. My uncle was always shabbily dressed, with a thin delicate-looking face covered with scaly skin, and though several years older than my father, still had his full jet-black hair.

The fact that he always turned around and left just before the argument was at its peak, even though he did it humbly, enraged my father. "He knew that I would prove him wrong, that is why he left; that is why he always leaves. He knew he had no show, so he did not want to stay and hear it," my father would say.

But it seemed to me that every time my uncle spoke, he always had a show. He was that kind of character, my uncle. But then, I had not seen his land yet. I did not yet know the conditions, nor the tremendous odds my uncle was up against.

Once, however, my uncle was caught in the middle of an argument. It was the time when the party was thrown in our house by the parents for their children who were graduating from elementary school, two weeks before the final examinations. I was one of them, and my father was the host. My uncle had come from his farm to congratulate me, and besides that, we had not seen each other for some time.

When I saw that *caretella* coming down the hill, that one-horse cart, I knew it was he. When he arrived, he paid his respects to everyone, and then we went to the patio on the back of the house, and he sat down on a bench.

"And how are you, my nephew?" He waved his hat downwards to me. "Sit down."

Smiling, I sat down on a rattan chair opposite him. "Well, my uncle," I said, not knowing what else to say.

"I have no gift to bring you—"

"You are here," I said.

"Well, yes, but is it not customary to . . . however, since I have no gifts, could we have a talk instead?"

"About what?"

"Oh, about things—perhaps of importance to you, since you are now graduating."

"Oh," I said, a bit disappointed.

"No, no. It is not advice, my nephew," he laughed. "I know you are filled with it by now."

"What, then?" I looked up at him. "What is it?"

I could see he was in agony trying to tell me something. Sitting back, I let him take his time.

"My nephew," he began, "you know you have always had this—how shall I say it—this heart of a poet. . . ."

I heard the clatter of feet from inside, the sound of laughter, and soon, as I half dreaded, I heard them call my name. The patio door suddenly opened and my father had his hand in mine, dragging me inside. "The guests have arrived, Amador!" he said. I had to join and mix with the people because I was supposed to be the valedictorian, but before I left my uncle, he told me that this time, no matter how heated any argument with my father or anybody else became, he would not leave until he was sure I had some notion of that thing he was trying to tell me earlier when we were interrupted.

Therefore, this time my uncle did not leave but stood his ground. He stood chin up, one hand in his pocket, the other on his bamboo pipe, answering my father repeatedly with only two words:

"I refuse," he kept saying. They spoke to each other from a distance; they always did.

"But why? What good is that land of yours? It is barren, brother. It is fungus-ridden; it is craggy and rocky. It is lifeless and grows nothing and yields nothing. Everyone on the Board already ridicules me about it."

My father spoke very fluent Tagalog, the national dialect, even though they originally spoke a provincial tongue. He had already lost the provincial dialect accent. My uncle was the other way. He spoke the national tongue with a thick provincial accent. And I, born in the *barrio* and raised in the cities of Manila and Tacloban, was more familiar with the national tongue. I understood both, but my father and I had to feel for words when talking to my uncle.

My father continued, "Why do you not sell it to the community, Andres? They are going to get it sooner or later, so you can at least have a financial hold and stop being a worthless vagabond all your life, a bum!"

"I do not beg, brother," said my uncle, "nor do I sell."

"I know you do not beg; but at least invest in something that stands fast. Your land is nothing."

"Nothing stands faster than the land."

"But your land is nothing."

"It does not have to be anything. It is everlasting," my uncle said, and lowering his voice he added, "and I refuse to sell it."

"What is wrong? They offer a price high enough for it," my father said. He was also a member of the Board.

"Price indeed is too high."

"Then why not take it?"

"I talk of the price of accepting their offer."

I could tell my father was already getting excited. He had begun crushing the tip of his cigarette filter with his thumbnail, pressing crisscross lines of all sorts. "Did you know," he said, pointing at my uncle with the two fingers that held his cigarette, "did you know that people like you have no place in the world? No place whatsoever."

My uncle struck a match against his teeth and lit his pipe. "I can't help it."

"I think you're in love with being a bum. Why can you not live like other people?" my father shouted.

"The price. It is the price." My uncle whispered, looking at me. I felt his eyes. He faced my father, but his eyes were speaking to me.

Right after that argument Uncle Andres took me for a ride in his old buggy-cart to his place that the community could not buy. The ride was fun. We, that is, my father, owned a car, but I rarely had horse-cart rides. As we left, we saw my father standing in the middle of the dirt road getting smaller and smaller, for the horse was now in full gallop.

"He is a good man," I said, "but he has not much faith, my uncle."

"Faith in me, you mean."

"Well . . . just faith. He has not much of it."

"It is not a question of faith, my nephew. But still you are right. He is truly a good man. A man of prudence."

"But so are you—in a way. You are a man of vision."

"It is my bad luck," he smiled. I thought his face, so brittle-looking and scaly, would fall to pieces.

"Why is it father always talks to you like that?" I asked him. "I mean, you are older, are you not? He never lets me talk to Bong like that." Bong was my older brother.

I did not think he heard me, for he said nothing. Then he suddenly released the reins and stopped the cart. "Hey, did I ever tell you the story of the guitar and how it all came about?"

He had told it to me at least three times before, but I could see from his face that he had forgotten. He looked so eager to tell it, so I said no, he had not.

And he told me again. It was about how a young lad a long time ago was banished from his village in Spain because he had leprosy. This young man used to sing love songs in the marketplace. He sang them one after the other, wanted to sing them all, for he knew he did not have much time left and the people would ostracize him sooner or later.

And they did, for the lady in his songs felt very insulted. She and her parents—they were aristocrats—organized a board of some sort and ordered the leper out. He refused, until the lady herself confronted him (from a distance, of course) in front of the marketplace and told him how disgusting and revolting he looked, and how dared he even think of her existence. The leper turned around, left town, and was never seen by any of them again.

But he hid himself in the hills and lived in a cave there. He carved out a hollow tree in the shape of a woman's body. He made her neck long and slender so that he could stroke it and caress it as his hand glided over it. And every time he held the thing, he would imagine his arm embracing her tender waist. Finally he bored a hole where the heart should be and connected strings from there to her lips above her neck. Her lips he manipulated with his fingertips, and as he plucked, he imagined the strings to be of her heart, as if their destiny depended on the singing of his song and the playing of his guitar.

Of course, I did not believe him. But it is strange, because while he told it, I did. But only while he was telling it. Right after, once I started thinking about it, I could not believe it any more. It just could not be. But I believed him, knowing it was a lie. It was so pretty, the way he told it.

My uncle started the *caretella* again. "I will show you the land, Amador. And I will tell you what we will make of it."

"How do you mean, *we*? I know nothing of the land." I was only in the eighth grade.

"I will teach you," he said. "I realize it is not much, but we will make it bloom just the same. With thousands of apple trees!"

"You are going to make a farm out of it? Apple trees don't grow here. Climate does not allow it, my uncle."

"Farm? We will make a *garden* out of it!" he whispered with fury, arms outstretched. "Apple trees, hyacinth bushes, jasmines, sampaguitas, and of course, there is always the lotus. But apples will be the main crop."

I was confused.

"Did you know, Amador, that you are the only one I have ever brought out here to see the land?" he said.

I had a feeling I was, but I said no, I did not.

"Yes, you are," he said, looking at the low dry sky. I guess he thought that I was the only one he could find that somehow understood his unquenchable impulse to plant the land and see it grow, understood the majesty of the force that was driving him to magnificent ruin. I remembered he had called me a poet at heart, once.

When we got to his place, I was horrified at the sight. There was not even a slight breeze to stir the carpeting dust. Where there was no dust, rocks stood, already cracked by the heat. From where I stood I could see no sign of water. Only rocks and dust and parched scales or cracked earth stared at me. Father was right about it.

"Why do you pick such a time of all time, the dry season, to plant, my uncle? Why not wait till the rainy season; at least you will have a chance then?" I was more and more convinced I knew more of farming than he did.

"Because they are after me, my boy. By then they will surely have taken this land and built apartments on it or used it as a garbage dump or a golf course. But I will show them. They just do not see the beauty in it . . . and you will help me, won't you?"

"Sure," I heard my lips say. I think it was the land that made my uncle look so fragile and vulnerable. He sounded so intense and desperate every time he spoke to me about it.

"Father said they will get it sooner or later."

My uncle laughed and said, "When this garden blooms, Amador, everyone all over southeast Asia will come just to get a whiff of it. It will be a shrine for everything and anything they want it to stand for. In its majesty it will overshadow the Taj Mahal, and of its beauty poets shall sing, and of its divinity prayers will be offered!" For a moment his face was lit up by that vision.

I looked once more at the stretched-out, thin-layered, scaly-cracked earth. "Father says it yields nothing. Everybody says it is lifeless."

He looked at me limply and said, "I refuse to believe

that. The life of the land is preserved by its righteousness."

I was frightened when he spoke in that way, in that frail tone. Frightened because he sounded so helpless that I was filled with an overwhelming passion to stand by him no matter what, and at the same time filled with the certainty that we, my uncle and I, would be crushed just the same. It was then that I knew the reason for my uncle's fragility, and the inevitable, gloriously tragic consequences of that fragility. For I had seen my uncle's land, and the futility of it all.

We walked slowly on the land, threshing the dust and kicking the rocks as we passed. A lizard scurried by, and I stepped on it lightly to pin it down. Then I picked it up.

"What is that?" he asked.

"A lizard."

"Does it bite?"

"No."

"Is it harmful?"

"No, my uncle, but it is a bad sign."

"For farming?"

"For anything. It is bad luck."

"Are there plenty of them around?"

"The place is crawling with them," I said.

"But is it bad for farming?"

"For anything, I told you."

We walked some more until finally my uncle headed back. Far off, on the crest of a hill, my uncle's small shack could be seen emerging, while the sun, directly behind it, sank slowly. Looking towards that hill, he put his arm gently around my shoulder, but somehow his arm seemed heavier than lead. And I could not speak. I could feel something coming, as if a pebble had dropped into a well and no sound came. I waited.

"You know, Amador," he began. Still too intense to speak. I could tell he was trying hard to explain something. I could feel the stiff grizzly hair of his hand against my cheek. He spoke slowly and carefully.

"You know . . . the mango trees . . . see them there, below that hill? And the lotus in the fields . . . somehow mean more to me now, are closer to me now. More than they do for most people, I suppose. You see, Amador . . . my whole life has been an apology. And all I want now is to be cradled in everybody's arms. Yet—" he stopped. And realizing he could not finish that train of thought, went on to another. The sun was blood-red now, and the hill where my uncle's house rested stood dripping scarlet. The whole landscape pulsated, red with fire.

"My nephew, I grow old and silly," he continued. "I am childless . . . and wifeless . . . and homeless. I grow old and I grow old. Things left to hang on to are getting fewer and fewer. . . ."

"Yes," was all I could answer. "Yes, my uncle, I see."

His words ran shrieking through me; a chalk had scraped along the blackboard, and the sound flashed like lightning down my spine.

"I will clear everything with your father and the Board tomorrow," he smiled.

He was still smiling in the Board office the next afternoon. He shook hands with everyone, and everyone smiled back. But I could feel them all looking at my father.

"Why did you bring the boy?" my father asked my uncle.

"I wanted him along."

"Did you go to school today?"

"Yes, I've finished, father," I said, rising.

"Did you know this is his last two weeks? He has examinations, you know." He turned to my uncle.

"He did not mention it." He looked at me; I looked quickly away.

"Hmmm." My father looked at his watch. "Well, are you finally handing it over to us?"

"No," my uncle said. "I am going to cultivate it. I've bought all the equipment. All I need is your signatures"—he looked around at the Board members—"giving me till at least the rainy season, that's about a month from now, to grow something on it."

The usual argument broke out again. My father got redder and redder, and he began making the crisscross lines on the cigarette filter with his thumbnail. While my uncle's words got fewer and fewer until at last they were down to two again: "I refuse," shaking his scaly-skinned head. "I refuse," he kept repeating until they gave him at last his show. Until the beginning of the rainy season; then, if still nothing grew, my uncle's land would be sold to my father and the Board.

My uncle went his way and we, my father and I, went ours. It was a very quiet drive home. The silence was painful, but my father, with some restraint, finally broke it.

"So, you are going to help him," he said.

"I do not know."

"What do you mean, do not know? I can tell you are, my son. You *want* to help him, let us put it that way."

"Yes," I answered.

"What about your schoolwork? I mean, how will you study? The examinations are only two weeks away. You simply do not have the time, you know."

I said I knew.

"But how are you going to manage? You and your uncle do not know it yet, but it is going to take the devil's zeal to work it. You are very good in school. I hate to see your marks drop just when you are going to graduate."

"They will not drop very much."

"You have seen the land, have you not?" My father laughed dryly.

I said yes; I had seen the land.

"You fools! You really think you have a chance?" He raised his voice and knitted his brow. He was looking at me now more than he was looking at the road. The lights from the lampposts filtered through the trees and flashed now on his face, now on his profile. "Listen," he said. The flickering lights made him look so distraught and intense. I had never seen him like that before. He tilted his head and squinted his eyes, as if he were having great difficulty in speaking.

"You are my only hope, my son," he said. "Bong has quit school. Don't tell me you will too." His voice threatened to break, but he checked himself instantly. "Amador, I know you are quite fond of your uncle . . . I envy him at times. No, no, no, don't apologize for it, my son. We are

different, your uncle and I, no need to apologize for that."
After an awkward pause, he continued with a hesitant
smile, "That is why for you I will help him too."

"How?"

"I will purchase him some other piece of land, a much
better piece, from the money he gets for this one. I know
some people, and I will personally see to it that—"

"I do not think he will allow it, my father."

"Of course he will. He must."

"You know him. It is not his way."

"Then we will make it his way!" He flicked his cigarette
out of the window. "I do not care whether it is your uncle
or the Community Board who gets the land or not, the
devil take them both! They are nothing to me. But you are
my son. And you are my pride. And I know as well as you
that you will not graduate if you plow the fields with your
Uncle Andres."

"He will be destroyed," I pleaded.

"He will be crushed whether you help him or not," he
answered quickly. "He hasn't a chance, the old fool. Tell
him to dream another dream. Do you really think he has a
chance?"

I said I did not think so.

"Then why help him?"

I said I still did not know if I should help him, but I
wanted to just the same.

"Why, why do you want to just the same?"

I tried to say something, but nothing came out. "I do not
know," I said.

The car stopped. My father opened his door, shut it, and
then opened mine. "Come out. We're home," I heard him
say.

Snapping out of my thoughts, I jumped out. His hand was
waiting outside to take mine. He pushed the gate open,
and we walked along the cement path towards the door. I
gently released my hand from his.

"Are you not coming in, my son?" He forced a smile that
made me feel very cruel.

The next day my uncle, still smiling, came to the house to get me. He was so sure I would go. I would be gone about four weeks and commute to school from my uncle's place to finish the semester. Paying his respects to all, he looked up to me as I was coming down the stairs with my luggage.

"Got everything, eh? Don't forget your books now." He laughed and turned to my father, who was looking at me in silence.

I nodded I had them.

My father and I did not speak a word, and both of us felt the weight of our silence. We had felt it last night when I left him to take a walk alone just before supper. And when I heard him downstairs this morning listening to me pack, I knew he would not go to work that day.

Uncle Andres waved good-bye to everyone, and he was already on the one-horse cart when I got to the door. Opening it and putting my luggage across the threshold, I eyed my father good-bye; he did not move.

Scattered rains had already begun. Uncle Andres drove me to school every day and then picked me up afterwards. After school I studied a while, then worked with my uncle for four or six hours. My father was right. It was a lot of work. But my uncle and I stayed with it for the whole two weeks just the same. My grades dropped more than I had expected. I did not make valedictorian, of course, nor anywhere near it. I did not graduate that year. And if my uncle was a poor farmer, with a thin delicate body, he made up for it with his diligence. He checked and rechecked and replaced every ruined seedling and changed its coverings all through the winds and rains and mud.

I lived in my uncle's shack and waited with him for three more weeks before the preliminary rains were over. When the winds had finally died and the sky started to clear, he dressed in his finest suit. He was running up and down the house getting ready to "greet the flowering fields."

"Hey, don't just stand there. Where's *your* suit?"

"In my suitcase," I smiled. "Don't tell me—"

"That's right. Go put it on, boy. You're in the parade too.

You and I worked this land, remember?"

"How can I forget."

"Come, my nephew. Do not try to hide emotions from me. It is only me. I know you feel it too." He fixed a button-hole. "I feel like a whale lifting the sea," he puffed. "Or a bird moving the wind. Or the mountains rising with the morning!" He turned and caught me smiling. "That's it. Laugh! Don't hold back that smile. I know you feel it too."

He was right; I felt it too.

We hopped on the *caretella* and whipped the old mare. "To the flowering fields!" he shouted.

When we got there, we saw nothing.

Nothing. Not even a single seedling had pierced through its covering. They were all blown by the winds or suffocated by the thick mud that had already begun to harden and crack anew in the sun. We walked some more, a little slower this time, my uncle's face sunken and bent, but still found nothing.

"I think it is time that I go," he whimpered. "I must leave, leave."

I started groping desperately for words. My uncle looked like a stranger already. There was too much to say, and I felt the difference in dialects growing thicker than ever, felt we were two minstrels that had sung all the songs and played every tune in the world, only to realize afterwards that no one was listening.

FOR DISCUSSION

1. What does land mean to Uncle Andres? What does it mean to the boy in the story?

2. What does Uncle Andres mean when he says, "The life of the land is preserved by its righteousness"?